OPPORTUNITIES IN
Real Estate
Careers

MARIWYN EVANS

Foreword by
Richard Mendenhall
President
National Association of REALTORS®

VGM Career Books
*Chicago   New York   San Francisco   Lisbon   London   Madrid   Mexico City
Milan   New Delhi   San Juan   Seoul   Singapore   Sydney   Toronto*

Library of Congress Cataloging-in-Publication Data

Evans, Mariwyn.
    Opportunities in real estate careers / Mariwyn Evans ; foreword by
Richard Mendenhall—Rev. ed.
        p. cm.—(VGM opportunities series)
    Includes bibliographical references.
    ISBN 0-07-138714-5 (hardcover)
    ISBN 0-07-138715-3 (paperback)
    1. Real estate business—Vocational guidance. I. Title: Real estate
career. II. Title. III. Series.

HD1382.E9   2002
333.3'023'73—dc21

                                          2001055936

VGM Career Books

A Division of The McGraw-Hill Companies

2 3 4 5 6 7 8 9 0   LBM/LBM   1 0 9 8 7 6 5 4 3

ISBN 0-07-138714-5 (hardcover)
ISBN 0-07-138715-3 (paperback)

This book was set in Adobe Garamond by Rattray Design
Printed and bound by Lake Book Manufacturing

Cover photograph copyright © PhotoDisc

McGraw-Hill books are available at special quantity discounts to use as
premiums and sales promotions, or for use in corporate training programs. For
more information, please write to the Director of Special Sales, Professional
Publishing, McGraw-Hill, Two Penn Plaza, New York, NY 10121-2298. Or
contact your local bookstore.

This book is printed on acid-free paper.

Contents

iii

8. The Real Estate Business Today 147

The move toward a national real estate industry.
A changing real estate climate. The growth of
technology. The future of real estate.

FOREWORD

A CENTURY AGO in the United States, only 8 percent of the homes had a telephone and only 14 percent had a bathtub. More than 95 percent of all births in the United States took place at home. Antibiotics had not been invented, and a person's average life span was forty-seven years. The leading causes of death were pneumonia, influenza, and tuberculosis. The average worker made less than $500 per year, and only 6 percent of seventeen-year-olds had graduated from high school. There were only ten miles of paved roads. Scotch tape, crossword puzzles, canned beer, and iced tea were unknown. The population of Las Vegas, Nevada, was nineteen—maybe thirty on a good day. And a U.S. postage stamp cost two cents.

So why are things so different today? True, a lot of things have happened to our quality of life in the past one hundred years—some good, some not so good. But what caused all the changes to happen? There is only one answer—people. People with a purpose. People who set a goal, made a commitment, and caused something to happen. I believe that the driving force behind all of that innovation and success is a great education and people who continue to educate themselves and believe in themselves.

My mother, who is the fourth generation in our family in real estate, said, "Success in real estate is a four-letter word—guts!" When I first got my real estate license, my mother, then already a realtor, told me that I must continue to attend education courses. To her it was not optional. And, of course, she was right. It meant all the difference in the world to my real estate career. The question was where would I get the education for my career. Well, it happens that organized real estate has some of the best career education in the world. It covers all kinds of topics and issues and is available everywhere and all the time. Today you can even get really good education to help you do your job better on the Internet and through satellite TV. There is just no industry like it.

If you have the will and interest, the opportunity is available for men and women alike to be very successful in a real estate career.

Richard Mendenhall
President
National Association of REALTORS®

1

A Summary of the Real Estate Field

The real estate industry helps individuals and companies buy, sell, lease, manage, and evaluate property. Often people have the idea that real estate agents are concerned only with buying and selling homes and condominiums. And they are right—at least up to a point. Approximately 76 percent of real estate firms work primarily in the residential real estate market. But that is only one area of the diversified real estate business. Real estate agents help others buy and sell residential, agricultural, commercial, and industrial properties; lease and manage office buildings, shopping centers, and apartment buildings; oversee real estate on behalf of banks, pension funds, and publicly traded real estate companies; and evaluate properties for individuals, banks, and insurance companies. Real estate professionals develop land, plan real estate investments, and help arrange financing for property.

Real estate agents work in all types of environments. Many residential real estate firms employ fewer than ten people, while large development companies may build hundreds of housing units or huge shopping centers, thus requiring hundreds of employees. Other agents choose to concentrate on one of the specialized areas of real estate such as appraising, property management, or commercial leasing. There are also many fields closely allied to the real estate industry that offer employment to those who have an interest in real estate. Lawyers, builders, and mortgage officers all work closely with real estate agents. Real estate closers, escrow agents, and title researchers handle important elements of the real estate transaction. Wall Street analysts assess the performance of real estate–related stocks.

Real estate agents play a fundamental part in the use and exchange of one of this country's most important resources—real property. The industry offers a wide variety of opportunities to men and women of all ages and backgrounds. Advancement is limited only by an individual's determination and interests.

In this book we will explore some of the areas of specialization open to the prospective real estate agent. We also will describe some of the typical activities of a real estate agent and discuss educational and other requirements for entering the field. Finally we will look toward the future and try to predict what the real estate business and real estate agents will be like in the years to come.

Real Estate Ownership

For legal purposes, real estate is defined as land and all the natural and man-made improvements attached to that land. An improvement is anything that is permanently attached to property, such as trees, buildings, or roads. When you buy or sell real estate, you usually buy both the land and the improvements. But you do not just buy the land and the buildings. Real estate usually also encompasses the rights to all of the air above the property and to the minerals and water underneath the property. This means that when you buy property, you also buy the rights to all of the oil, minerals, and water that are under your property. Likewise, with the exception of rights for airplanes and utilities, you also buy the rights to the airspace above your property. In fact, when a person buys an apartment in a high-rise building, he or she is actually buying part of the airspace that belonged to the land's owner.

The example above illustrates an interesting legal point about property ownership. Although most buyers purchase all of the elements that are a part of the real estate, it is possible to buy or sell only one of these elements. For example, a property owner can sell the oil or mineral rights to a property and still keep the ownership rights to the land itself. There are actually brokers who specialize in buying and selling mineral rights.

Historical Overview of the Real Estate Field

Like many other transactions in our society, real estate sales are governed by a series of laws and regulations. These laws developed gradually to meet the needs of the society.

Property Law

In primitive societies, property was often owned and farmed by the tribe as a whole. Families of several generations lived in the same house, and property passed naturally from parents to children. During the Middle Ages, great nobles consolidated their power and gained control of large tracts of land. To administer these holdings, the nobles granted the use of the property to lesser nobles in return for loyalty and service. However, under this so-called feudal system, the nobles still owned the property; the landholders had only the use of the property for their lifetimes. When they died, the use of the land returned to the noble.

By the seventeenth century, the feudal system had been replaced by the allodial system of land ownership. Under this system, individuals owned land outright. They were able to sell the property or to pass it to their descendants. The English colonists brought the allodial system to the Americas. After the Revolutionary War, Americans' rights to own and dispose of real property were guaranteed under the Bill of Rights. Real estate law has become much more complex in the last two hundred years. Federal, state, and local governments have enacted laws and regulations that control real estate transfers. However, real property law in the United States is still based on the allodial system to possess, dispose, and enjoy property.

The Real Estate Agent's Job

Just as property law has changed to reflect the needs of society, the real estate profession has come into existence to meet the demands of the people. In earlier times, most people lived in small communities for their entire lives. If property were transferred from one person to another, every member of the community knew about it. Even in colonial America, most people moved around very little. When settlers moved to unexplored areas, they established ownership rights by living and working on the land.

By the late 1800s, however, society in America had changed drastically. The settled areas of the United States extended from coast to coast, railroads and roads spanned the continent, and the population was about fifteen times larger than it had been in 1800. These changes made it much more likely for American citizens to find opportunities in new parts of the country and, therefore, less likely for them to know their neighbors. More and more real estate was bought and sold, and more and more often the buyers and sellers were strangers. These increased sales created a need for an individual who knew about property and was able to act as a trusted agent between strangers. At first the role of agent was performed by lawyers or other professionals, but gradually real estate emerged as a distinct field of expertise. Today there are more than 750,000 real estate agents in the United States and 66,000 in Canada engaged in helping businesses and individuals carry out their real estate transactions.

The Emergence of the National Association of REALTORS® (NAR)

The importance of the real estate profession was greatly increased by the founding of the National Association of REALTORS in 1908. Begun by a group of real estate agents, this trade organization was established to set standards of conduct for agents and to help increase public confidence in the real estate profession. Today the majority of real estate agents are members of the NAR (approximately 750,000 in 2000). The organization and its local chapters, or "boards," offer numerous courses and educational materials to help their members increase their professional abilities and also provide additional services such as information on trends in the industry. Other trade organizations such as the National Association of Real Estate Boards also conduct courses and provide services to their members. The Canadian Real Estate Association had more than 66,000 members in 2000.

Specialized courses are offered through a variety of associations such as the Appraisal Institute (appraisal), the Institute of Real Estate Management (property management), the Commercial-Investment Real Estate Institute (commercial brokerage), the Community Associations Institute (condominium management), the International Council of Shopping Centers (mall development and management), and the National Apartment Association (apartment development).

Many colleges and universities also offer graduate and undergraduate degrees in real estate, land-use planning, or urban economics.

Brokers and Salespeople

Although real estate agents can be engaged in a variety of jobs, all real estate agents are legally classified as either brokers or salespeople. These designations are set down in state real estate license laws. All states and the District of Columbia require real estate agents to be licensed in the state before they can work in the real estate business. Although state laws vary, most define a real estate broker as an individual who for compensation (money or other payment) buys, sells, leases, exchanges, evaluates, or otherwise negotiates a real estate transaction for another individual.

Most laws make certain exceptions to these requirements for licensure. For example, if you are selling or leasing real estate that you own, you usually do not have to be licensed. Some states also exempt on-site condominium management from licensure.

Under state laws, a salesperson also must be licensed if he or she performs any of the activities listed above. Salespeople dealing in Real Estate Investment Trusts (REITs) also may need a license from the Securities Exchange Commission. In addition, real estate salespeople are prohibited from engaging in the real estate business unless they work under the supervision of a licensed real estate broker. Usually salespeople have to meet fewer educational and experience requirements than brokers to receive a license.

Real Estate at Home and Abroad

Buying a home is often the largest investment of a person's life. With the median price of a U.S. home reaching $143,500 in the first quarter of 2001, this is more true than ever. The average price of an existing home in Canada was $177,817 (Canadian dollars) in April 2001. Home mortgages paid over a fifteen- to thirty-year period represent the work and savings of a lifetime. And the time and money most owners spend on their homes further increases the property's value.

Despite higher home prices, low mortgage interest rates and rising personal income have helped home ownership remain affordable for the average American. In the first quarter of 2001, the National Association of REALTORS' "Housing Affordability Index" had risen 9.2 percent over 2000 levels. In early 2001, NAR found that the average family would have 42.9 percent more income than was needed to obtain an 80 percent mortgage and buy the averaged-price home. In this survey, housing was most affordable in the Midwest and least affordable in the West.

Real estate is also important in that it represents a greater than 50 percent segment of the U.S. economy. For this reason, the real estate market is strongly influenced by the condition of the American economy as a whole.

Housing starts have remained strong in the United States with approximately 1.67 million new starts in early 2001. In Canada,

1995 saw 147,000 new starts and sluggish sales because of continued concerns over slow economic growth. Houses in both countries are getting larger, with more bedrooms, more bathrooms, and more amenities. According to the National Association of Home Builders, the average size of a new U.S. home in 2001 was more than two thousand square feet.

Office and industrial construction has been moderate in the United States in the last few years, as banks and other lenders have kept a tight rein on funds. As a result, office vacancies have been below 10 percent in most markets and rents have risen significantly over the last few years. Although recent economic slowdowns have created some concern and somewhat higher vacancies, most experts believe that thanks to a limited supply, office and industrial rents will remain fairly stable in the early 2000s.

Both the United States and Canada predict growth rates of between 2 and 4 percent for the next two or three years, with low inflation. If these predictions are accurate, demand for all types of real estate should remain stable.

Tax laws and other government policies also have an effect on the real estate market. Federal tax laws that allow for substantial deductions for mortgage interest payments and the cost of real estate purchases encourage real estate construction and investment by individuals. Currently, real estate is a favored investment for tax purposes in the United States because home owners and many commercial owners can deduct interest and property taxes from their overall income. This makes home ownership more feasible for many families. Some real estate professionals are concerned that discussions of flat tax proposals may eliminate or reduce this deduction. However, sales thus far have not been affected.

In Canada, high property taxes in several provinces are having a negative effect on real estate values.

Although the real estate market tends to fluctuate more than do many other industries, there will always be a demand for real estate. For most people, home ownership is still a desirable goal. As long as there is a demand for real estate, there will be a demand for real estate brokers and salespeople to help people meet their needs.

Real Estate and the Web

Perhaps no single factor has had a more significant change on the real estate industry than computerization and the use of the Internet to transfer information. The Research Institute for Housing in America found that in 2000, 75 percent of home buyers used the Internet to check mortgage rates, and 17 percent actually obtained their loans via the Internet. Likewise, the *NAR 2000 Profile of Home Buyers and Home Sellers* found that 37 percent of home buyers first investigated homes on the Internet. However, 87 percent of those home buyers still used a real estate agent in making their transaction.

Nor is the effect of technology limited to consumers. Real estate developers and builders can transfer building drawings and bids via the Web to save time and money in the construction process. Real estate agents now can access home listings from an Internet service on their laptops or even on their personal digital assistants, and then E-mail housing information to clients. Far-flung international companies can use private intranets to oversee properties in Singapore and Paris. Management companies have developed private websites for their building tenants to make it easier to request repair services or to stay up to date on community activities. Several companies, including the NAR, are working to develop complete "transaction management platforms," which will allow all aspects of a typical real estate transaction to be conducted electronically.

2

A Look at the Industry*

Just as there is not only one real estate job, there is not only one type of person who can succeed in the real estate field. The characteristics that make a good property manager are not the same as those that make a good residential salesperson. For this reason almost anyone can find some area of specialization in the real estate industry that will match his or her abilities and interests. In this chapter we will explore some of the characteristics of the successful real estate agent.

As we recall from Chapter 1, real estate agents are divided into two major categories—brokers and salespeople. Most people begin their real estate careers as salespeople, and the career span of a real

---

*Unless otherwise specified, all the statistics that are cited in this chapter are taken from the *2001 Membership Profile* published by the National Association of REALTORS. Canadian information was based on a 1998 member survey by the Canadian Real Estate Association.

estate salesperson may be as little as one month or as much as twenty years. To work as a salesperson, an individual must hold a salesperson's license from the state where he or she lives. Even after they are licensed, real estate salespeople cannot engage in the real estate business unless they are associated with a licensed real estate broker.

The real estate broker oversees the activities of the salespeople with whom he or she is associated. Real estate brokers must meet more advanced educational requirements than salespeople and in most states, must have been in the real estate business for a certain number of years. Any person who operates his or her own firm must hold a real estate broker's license.

A Diversified Profession

Background

More than many other occupations, people enter real estate from different backgrounds and with different goals. To some extent this is because of the relative ease of entering the real estate field. Although all states now require a high school diploma or its equivalent for licensure, a college degree is not required. For this reason many people who cannot afford or are not interested in pursuing higher education find real estate an attractive career option. Another reason for the diversity in the profession is the large number of agents who select real estate as a second career. Many begin working in real estate on a part-time basis to supplement their regular incomes and find real estate a stimulating and rewarding career. Other agents turn to real estate when they find that their earlier jobs did not supply sufficient income or challenge. Others are attracted to the real estate field because it offers the opportunity for self-employment. Overall, eight out of every ten brokers and nine out of every ten salespeople have worked in another occupation before entering real estate.

Education

As with any other profession you might choose, a good education is important for success in real estate. All fifty states require real estate agents to be high school graduates or to hold an equivalency certificate. However, the trend in real estate is more and more toward a college educated sales force. In the National Association of REALTORS (NAR) survey of 1978, only 58 percent of its members had at least some college degree work. By 2001 this number had risen to 67 percent, with 23 percent having completed at least some graduate study. However, the number of brokers with a four-year college degree declined slightly from its high of 37 percent in 1984: For real estate salespeople, 72 percent of the NAR membership had completed college, while another 16 percent had gone on with graduate work.

For brokers in a 1993 study, the most common area of college study was business administration. About 36 percent of the brokers held degrees in business, while only about 12 percent held college degrees in liberal arts. About 12 percent of the brokers gave real estate as their college major.

Business administration also accounted for the largest number of college majors among salespeople (33 percent). Other fields of study for real estate salespeople include liberal arts and education. About 8 percent had majors in real estate.

Although real estate agents enter the profession with degrees in almost every specialty from economics to agriculture, it is clear that courses in financing, economics, marketing, and other business topics are seen as the most helpful to those considering real estate careers. As real estate majors become more prevalent and younger agents continue to enter the field, more agents are likely to hold real estate majors. And for those considering more demanding careers in appraisal, finance, or counseling, an advanced degree in a real estate specialty may become more common.

In addition to college educations, most real estate agents have taken one or more professional courses in real estate. In fact many states require that agents take a set number of hours before they can obtain a real estate license. Licensing requirements and education will be discussed in Chapter 3.

Brokers and salespeople also hold a variety of professional designations showing expertise in a real estate field. In 2001, 80 percent of brokers and 32 percent of salespeople held designations. Of that group approximately 35 percent of brokers held or were working toward the GRI (Graduate, Realtor Institute) designation. Other popular designations with brokers were Certified Residential Specialist (20 percent) and Certified Real Estate Brokerage Manager (62 percent).

Over 14 percent of salespeople in the 2001 NAR survey held the GRI designation, and 9 percent either held or were working toward the Accredited Buyer Representatives' designation.

Age

As might be expected, since real estate agents often are employed in other fields before entering real estate, the median age of real estate brokers is high—52 years—with the majority of brokers in the 45 to 59 age range. While there are only 3 percent of brokers in the age 29 or younger category, 16 percent are still active at age 64 or older.

The median age for salespeople is 50 years. Approximately 5 percent of the sales force are age 29 or younger, with the largest percentage in the 40 to 59 age range. The average age of a Canadian real estate agent was 48, up from 47 in 1995.

Earnings

Most real estate brokers and salespeople receive between 50 to 60 percent of commissions earned, with the remainder going to the brokerage company to cover expenses. About one-fifth of agents earn 100 percent commissions and pay all their own business expenses.

As many people do not enter real estate directly from school, it is difficult to make a comparison between an agent's age and his or her earnings. However, as in most occupations, earnings do increase with experience. According to the 2001 NAR survey, the average broker had a gross personal income of $47,700, an increase of 10 percent over 1998. The 1999 *Occupational Outlook Handbook* pegged the average salary for a salesperson at $28,020. Median gross personal earnings for all brokers with one to five years of experience averaged $38,800; for those with eleven to fifteen years of experience, $74,300, in 2001. Twenty-three percent of brokers in the NAR survey earned more than $100,000.

Canadian agents and brokers averaged earnings of between $28,000 and $56,000 (Canadian dollars). The latest Census of Population conducted by the Canadian government showed an average salary of $40,471 for real estate agents.

Earnings also will vary depending on an agent's area of specialization. Agents in development or management average higher earnings while those in the residential area average the lowest. Salaries for different specialties will be discussed in Chapter 6.

There is the same correlation between experience and earnings for salespeople. In 2001 the real estate salesperson who had been in the business for one to five years earned a median net salary of $18,800 annually. Those salespeople in the business eleven to fifteen years earned a median of $44,900. Sixty-four percent of part-time salespeople had a median income of less than $10,000 per year.

Hours

Brokers and salespeople have traditionally put in long hours, and the trend seems to be increasing. In 2000 the typical broker worked forty-five hours per week, and 13 percent worked sixty hours or more. Salespeople worked a median of forty-one hours per week, with 8 percent working sixty or more hours. Only 14 percent of salespeople worked part-time.

Ownership Interest

In 2000, 41 percent of brokers had some sort of ownership interest in their firms. Approximately 20 percent of the brokers questioned in the 2001 NAR survey owned their own businesses, and another 18 percent owned either a partnership or corporate interest. Salespeople are not allowed to own a real estate business under most state license laws, but some do hold stock interest in their firms. However, in 2000 the NAR survey found that 95 percent of salespeople worked as independent contractors.

The average Canadian real estate agent worked for a firm with thirty-six members, up from twenty-eight in 1991.

Experience

The average real estate agent in the 2001 NAR survey has been in the real estate business for a median of thirteen years. Brokers who belong to NAR have been in the real estate business a median of twenty years. Approximately 63 percent of brokers have been in the business for more than sixteen years.

Opportunities for Women and Minorities

As much of the success in the real estate business depends on a person's ability to sell or list property, there are greater opportunities in real estate for women and minorities than there are in many other fields. Any person who can sell successfully can be certain of a job and reasonable earnings. And the opportunities are increasing every year. Approximately 56 percent of all real estate agents in the 2001 NAR survey were women. Approximately 46 percent of brokers were women in 2000. However, like many other fields, women and minorities will find that while they can succeed, their earnings will not usually be as high as those of white males.

Much of the cause for women's lower earnings is the result of their concentration in residential real estate sales. This traditionally women's field of selling single-family homes still accounts for most of the women in real estate. Also, more women work part-time than do men. Although it is certainly possible to earn a good living in residential sales, the earnings per transaction are usually lower than those in commercial or industrial transactions. In addition, the lucrative areas of commercial and industrial sales, as well as specialties such as mortgage banking and appraisal, have very few women participants. However, as more and more women enter specialty areas, the median income for them should rise.

Another problem that confronts women engaged in the real estate profession is their traditional role as the principal parent. The long and irregular hours worked by most salespeople make it extremely difficult for women to care for their children, especially if they are single parents. Women may find it difficult to work as many hours as their male counterparts, thereby lowering their overall earnings.

Unlike women, ethnic minorities tend to be poorly represented in the real estate profession. In the 2001 NAR survey, only 1 percent of respondents were African-American, 2 percent were Asian, and 5 percent were of Hispanic origin.

Because of the past and present discrimination, many African-Americans and other minorities have lower incomes than whites. They are more likely to be unable to buy their own homes, and the average price of these homes tends to be lower. Thus commission rates on these sales will be less than those for more expensive homes.

According to the *1999 NAR Profile of Real Estate Firms,* approximately 9 percent of real estate firms were at least partially owned by a member of a minority group. Nearly one-third of all firms have minority agents.

What Makes a Successful Real Estate Agent?

As we saw in Chapter 1, there are so many specialties in the real estate industry, it is difficult to select any one set of characteristics that will ensure success in the field. However, there are a few qualities that are necessary to almost every area of the business.

People-Oriented

Perhaps the most important quality that a prospective real estate agent should have is the ability to work with people. Real estate is essentially a service business. Obviously some jobs, such as sales, may take a higher level of people skills than more technical jobs, such as appraisal. But all brokers and salespeople work on behalf of one or more clients, and they need to be able to understand what clients want in order to perform their jobs.

Salespeople must be able to communicate with people on two different levels. First they must have a good knowledge of and interest in people. They must be able to understand the needs of the client and must learn to ask probing questions that help to point out the client's needs. To do this successfully, a broker or salesperson should have a real interest, beyond the financial rewards, in helping his or her clients meet their needs. Especially in the case of residential sales, there is a great deal of emotional involvement in the purchase of real estate. And the best salespeople are those who recognize this and become involved themselves. It really should matter whether the couple who buys the house will live happily there, not just whether they will sign the sales contract.

The other side of the need for communication skills in the real estate field is the ability to convince people of your opinions. Even though buying a house is a private decision, the real estate agent is the expert and should try to assist the client by giving him or her the benefit of expert knowledge. Many people find it difficult to make decisions on large or important purchases. Others are inclined to make a decision on emotional factors rather than on a realistic assessment of their needs. In such cases the real estate agent must use his or her people skills to gain the confidence of the parties and help to direct their decision. This need to establish themselves as reliable experts in the field is also an essential skill for those in other real estate areas. In all cases they must be able to convince their clients of their professionalism and clearly convey the knowledge that they have.

Detail-Oriented

Much of the real estate business is concerned with handling the small details correctly. It matters a great deal to the prospective buyer whether the house has been inspected for termites. The care a property manager uses to compute expenses can make the difference between a loss and a profit for the owners. Every real estate transaction involves contracts and affidavits that must be completed correctly if the sale is going to be legal. The successful real estate agent must be able to coordinate all of these elements. He or she also must be careful and conscientious enough to be sure that all the details are correct.

Enthusiastic

The last and perhaps the most important characteristic of a good real estate agent is enthusiasm. The agent must enjoy and be interested in the real estate field. The agent must believe in the importance of the job and in his or her ability to do it well. Without this certainty, the agent will find it difficult to convince prospective clients of his or her abilities. And sooner or later this lack of enthusiasm will make it hard for the agent to give his or her best to the job.

Of course, these are not the only qualities you need to succeed in real estate. Like many other professionals, real estate brokers and salespeople need to be mature, hardworking, intelligent, and honest. But if a real estate agent is going to move ahead in the field, he or she must be people-oriented, detail-minded, and enthusiastic.

The Advantages and Disadvantages of the Real Estate Business

Up to this point, we have focused on the advantages and rewards offered to those who choose real estate as a career. However, like any other business, there are some disadvantages to working in this field.

Flexibility in Scheduling

Because salespeople usually work as independent contractors rather than as employees, they can set their own work schedules. Even though brokers may ask that salespeople be in the office to cover the telephones during certain hours, salespeople are free to set up their own appointments with clients. This makes it easier to handle personal business and emergencies. But keep in mind that those who work fewer hours are likely to earn less.

The reverse side of this flexibility is that most agents' work schedules are both long and irregular. According to the 2001 NAR *Membership Survey*, the average real estate broker worked about forty-five hours a week with 10 percent putting in more than sixty hours. Residential brokers have to be available to show houses on weekends and in the evenings when other people are not working. And all real estate professionals must be prepared to provide services when the client wants them. Since it is a rare real estate broker who can work a traditional nine-to-five week, these irregular hours can place a strain on family relationships. Another pitfall is that since there are no definite hours for stopping work or taking vacations, many real estate agents develop the habit of working continually. In addition, because they are independent contractors, they are not paid for vacations and holidays, and so there is even less incentive to take time off.

One new trend in the real estate industry is a growing interest in having real estate agents work as salaried employees of the firm. Although this practice is much more common in specialties such as property management and appraisal, agents who work as employees in residential sales companies are on the rise, although they still account for only 3 percent of the sales force. For the agent, being an employee often means more regular hours, more regular income, and more fringe benefits. In some cases employees also will receive a bonus based on sales. Companies that use employee salespeople believe that *not* placing the agent in a position of earning a fee only if the sale closes promotes better customer service and more ethical conduct.

Irregular Income

Another mixed blessing in the real estate business is the irregularity of the income. Most real estate agents work on a commission basis, which means that their salaries depend on the number of sales they make. Although agents engaged in some specialties may receive a set salary, in most cases at least part of the income is based on commission. A commission is a percentage of the sales price, rental payment, or other fee that is paid to the person finalizing a transaction. Commission rates usually vary depending on the location and the type of specialty. Some agents are given a small monthly payment called a draw, which is charged against their future commissions. Some receive higher commission percentages as performance improves. Because salary is based on performance, the successful salesperson has the opportunity for unlimited earnings, restricted only by the time he or she has to spend on work.

However, because income is based on sales, there is not a set amount that the agent can count on receiving each month. Some months he or she will receive a large commission for a big sale while other months there will be little or no return for the hours worked. There is always some time-lapse between the time the sale is closed and the commission is received, which further increases the irregularity of the agent's income. This problem is particularly prevalent for those working in commercial and industrial broker-age, where it may take many months or years to complete one transaction. However, commissions for these transactions tend to be larger than those for residential sales.

This irregularity of income places a burden on the real estate agent to budget his or her money to allow for slow periods. In cases where the real estate field provides the family's sole source of income, it may be necessary to establish a substantial savings reserve to cover irregular income flow. People who have particu-lar difficulty adapting to the irregular income should consider working as a salaried employee in an area such as appraisal, where many agents work for institutions rather than as independent businesspeople.

Few Entry Requirements

A third advantage of the real estate profession is that unlike many other businesses there are very few requirements for entry into the field. All fifty states and the District of Columbia do require a high school degree or its equivalent. However, most states require only limited training before allowing a person to take the real estate licensing examination. (Educational requirements will be discussed further in Chapter 3.) Because of its limited educational demands, real estate is an attractive career choice for students who do not want to go to college or cannot afford the tuition. It also makes it easier for older people to enter the field without the need to return to school for an extended period. According to the 2001 NAR survey, only 7 percent of agents entered real estate as their first career.

Opportunities for Self-Employment

Many Americans dream of owning their own businesses, and this is a dream that was realized by 20 percent of the real estate brokers in the 2001 NAR survey. Since real estate is a service profession, brokers who want to go into business for themselves do not have the high capital outlays that are incurred in retailing or manufacturing. For this reason many brokers decide to set up their own firms after several years in the business. Although it is certainly appealing to be your own boss and have other people work for you, there are a great many problems in establishing and running a business. You will be able to hire salespeople and receive a portion of their commissions. However, you will have to devote a portion of your time to administrative duties and paperwork. This will limit the time you can sell and possibly reduce your own commission income. Also, the growing importance of computers in real estate transactions requires capital outlays for buying and upgrading technology. Because of real estate's irregular income flow, you will have to have cash reserves to live and pay the firm's expenses until commissions come in. In any case, even if setting up your own firm is a long-range goal, real estate agents should not consider this step until they have at least three to five years of sales experience.

A Cross Section of Careers

Over and over again we have made the point that the real estate field offers a variety of different jobs to many different types of people. In this section we will try to present brief portraits of men and women who have chosen real estate as their careers. You can see that although there are certain similarities in these people and their backgrounds, the differences far outweigh these similarities.

Juli Rojas—RE/MAX Properties Unlimited, Morristown, NJ

Although she thought real estate seemed like an interesting business, the then twenty-one-year-old Rojas didn't consider it a viable career because "everyone was older; it didn't seem like a business for a young person." Plus, she says, a lot of her friends and family didn't care for the idea. They all knew of someone who had tried their hand at real estate and failed, and they were quick to point out all the drawbacks—no regular salary, no benefits.

But when Rojas lost her financial aid, she decided to temporarily curtail her college career at Rider University and return to the local community college near her home in Montclair, New Jersey. After a stint working part-time in a day care center, her boyfriend encouraged her to give real estate a try.

Rojas began her career in 1999 as a residential sales associate with the Morristown office of Weichert Realty, a larger regional company. "Being able to start with a large company was a big advantage. I received training and I had a mentor I could turn to with questions," says Rojas. In just three weeks she had written her first sales contract. And by her second year in the business, her sales had reached $2.3 million.

But that first year was tough. Rojas worked as a baby-sitter two mornings a week to bring in money while she waited for her paychecks. However, she turned her problem into an advantage by selling homes to several of her baby-sitting clients.

Rojas made the move to RE/MAX in January of 2001. She loves being her own boss and making her own hours. She works a lot of evenings and weekends, but likes the flexibility. She also likes the opportunity to be up and away from her desk and to interact with people. "I've always been a people person," says Rojas, who had earlier considered a career as a teacher.

The toughest part of selling real estate, she says, is staying organized and getting all the transaction paperwork completed. "You also have to be patient and not let yourself get frustrated if things don't work out," she says. "You have to be persistent."

And was age an issue—when the average age of a real estate salesperson is forty-seven years old? According to Rojas, it isn't for her clients. They like her enthusiasm. "It was tgugher gaining the respect of the older salespeople in my office," says Rojas. But her knowledge and success gradually won them over.

Earl W. Fernelius, SRAP, ASA—Earl Fernelius, Inc., Birmingham, MI

While working as a residential real estate broker, Earl W. Fernelius found that a great many of his clients wanted appraisals of their properties. And, he said, "Since no one else wanted to monkey with the job, I did it." Thus began his career as a real estate appraiser. Like so many other real estate professionals, Fernelius's real estate career began in residential sales. After receiving a bachelor of science degree and a teaching certificate from Eastern

Michigan University, he taught school for one year. That summer, at the suggestion of the parents of one of his students, he sold real estate. At the end of the summer, he found that he had made more money than he got for teaching all year long. He gave up teaching for real estate.

Although he worked in residential sales for several years and still does some work in the area through his brokerage firm, the former teacher now spends about 95 percent of his time on appraisals and market and feasibility studies through Earl Fernelius, Inc. Along with the challenge of the specialty, Fernelius likes appraisal because there is less daily frustration than there is with selling. There is nothing worse, he reflects, than working with a client for a month and then having him or her buy a house from the owner. Even though he still works on a fee basis, he likes the idea that if you do a job, "you know you're going to get paid." Even then, Fernelius noted, many clients believe that since they are hiring you, the appraisal should say what they want it to say. But, Fernelius says, "You have to look at yourself as an impartial estimator of value." You can't be "winking at" the person who hired you to agree upon a price. To help preserve appraisers' impartiality, no semblance of advocacy is permitted.

Fernelius believes that there is a great future for young people in real estate appraisal. But, he admits, it is difficult getting started, and many young people are not willing or able to accept the low fees or salaries of the first few years. There are a few apprenticeship programs, but other appraisers don't have the time to devote to training new members of the profession.

Fernelius does his part toward helping prospective appraisers by teaching appraisal courses at the University of Michigan extension program and at Oakland Community College. He is also a member of the advisory board to the Oakland Community College real estate program and a lecturer on appraisal and professional standards for the National Association of REALTORS and the Society of Real Estate Appraisers. Fernelius serves as a vice governor for the Michigan region of the Society of Real Estate Appraisers. In the past he has served as president of the Oakland County Chapter of the Society of Real Estate Appraisers, vice president of the Michigan Association of Realtors, and president of the Birmingham-Bloomfield Board of Realtors.

Allen S. Pesmen—Managing General Partner, Bannockburn Park Concepts, Inc., Bannockburn, IL

Real estate development started as just a sideline to a successful law practice for Allen Pesmen. As the developments became larger, more successful, and more time consuming, he realized he could no longer perform two jobs at once. He chose to put his energy into real estate. Today Pesmen's law firm practice is strictly limited to services for his company's affiliates.

A native of Chicago, Pesmen received his law degree from the University of Illinois in 1960 and from 1960 through 1981 was principal of a law firm, which was eventually known as Pesmen & Weil, P.C. Although his practice was general and business related, Pesmen found that a significant amount of his work was in real estate, including zoning and annexation for development. In 1969 he began accumulating the first of ten parcels of land for future real estate development.

Pesmen's first project was an eighty-six-acre complex to house Bannockburn Lake Office Plaza, Bannockburn Green Retail Center, and Bannockburn Bath and Tennis Club in north suburban

Chicago. Construction began in 1978. The complex consists of office buildings carefully placed among landscaped wooded areas and artificial lakes, which create a sylvan setting far removed from the nearby expressways.

The buildings' parklike setting received wide acclaim and was innovative at the time for the area, but it was chosen by Pesmen because of his personal preference. "I felt people wanted to get away from the congestion and the frustrations of the inner city, just as I did after two decades in the heart of Chicago's financial district," he said. "At Bannockburn Lake, our tenants can picnic at the lake, stroll the nature trail, or use the facilities of our Bannockburn Bath and Tennis Club next door without sacrificing the institutional features of quality office space."

Today Pesmen's properties include the Bannockburn office complex; the neighboring Bannockburn Green Retail and Office Center, which won a Distinguished Building Award from the American Institute of Architects and a Gold Award from the Illinois Landscape Contractors Association; and the Doe Run Lodge resort and condominiums in southwestern Virginia along the Blue Ridge Parkway. His company employs approximately fifty people at the central office. Among them is his wife, Enid, who acts as property manager for several of the firm's development projects. Additional staff are employed at each of the properties.

Pesmen's real estate enterprise rests on the foundation of his accounting, legal, and financial knowledge and on considerable firsthand real estate experience—a foundation he believes is essential to long-term success. "Today," he says, "many young people are attracted to real estate as a career primarily because they read about the fortunes having been made by developers and syndicators. What they don't realize is that there are numerous pitfalls and no guarantees in real estate development. The real estate market is like a pendulum, swinging back and forth between opportunities and disasters. It takes experience and good banking contacts to recognize in which direction the real estate financial markets are going and to adjust to those changes. In addition it takes considerable luck and good fortune."

Sandra Dzinski—CPM, Vice President, Equitable Real Estate, Irvine, CA (Equitable Real Estate is a wholly owned subsidiary of The Equitable.)

"I really got into real estate because I went bowling," jokes Sandy Dzinski. A social sciences graduate from the Colorado State University, Dzinski found it difficult to find a challenging first job. When a friend told her about a secretarial job with a real estate developer, she decided to apply.

At first the position was mostly clerical, but Dzinski kept her eyes open and demonstrated her abilities. Soon she was assisting in the preparation of feasibility studies and client reports. "An entry-level position provides the opportunity to do more; to prove that you have the intelligence and the drive," she says.

Soon another company was looking for a property management trainee and offered Dzinski the job. The firm encouraged her to attend local and national Institute of Real Estate Management meetings and to take courses in property management. At the courses and meetings, she also made contact with other professionals in the field and shared solutions to common problems.

After six years working for these two smaller companies in the west, Dzinski joined Equitable Real Estate. With offices in fifteen cities, the firm's national perspective and presence gave her the opportunity to work with larger, more challenging properties and in addition, offered greater long-term financial rewards than smaller concerns.

After nine years with Equitable as a property and commercial leasing manager, Dzinski moved into the area of representing the company's real estate services to its institutional accounts. In this position she acts as a liaison between Equitable's real estate investment services and the large public pension funds that want, or have placed, real estate in their investment portfolios.

The job involves new responsibilities, a new learning curve, and a great deal of travel, but Dzinski believes that her property management background helps in her new position. "Property management is really a people business," she says. "And in my current role, the ability to listen and to understand how to respond to needs is fundamental."

The diversity and flexibility of the real estate field is one of the factors that attracts Dzinski. "A real estate career can move in many directions," she summarizes. "There are tremendous challenges, and every day is different and stimulating."

Jerline Lambert—President, Lambert's Realty, Chicago, IL

Certainly the real estate career of broker Jerline Lambert is a prime example of the opportunities in real estate and the equal importance of determination and luck in shaping an individual's life. Now the president of her own brokerage firm on Chicago's west side, Lambert cut short her education in the tenth grade to marry and have children. After her children were born, she began working as a secretary and completed her journalism degree and two and one-half years of business education courses at the Chicago Central YMCA College. She found that her secretarial position did not offer her the freedom or opportunity she wanted, but she did not have any idea what she wanted to do instead. At this point fate stepped in.

Looking at houses with her husband and a local real estate agent, she was so interested in the business and asked such intelligent questions that the broker suggested she come and work for him. After taking a number of real estate courses, she acquired her real estate license. Then, after working briefly in a dime store to get some sales experience (which she had never had), Lambert went to work for the broker. After about a year, Lambert went to work for another successful broker, Geraldine Wells. She chose to work for a woman, she said, because "women use different techniques than men in selling, and I wanted to learn how a successful woman did it." After two and one-half years of practice, Lambert decided she was ready to go out on her own and opened Lambert's Realty. The firm's single office handles residential, commercial, and property management work with the help of a few salespeople, including two of Lambert's children. Lambert decided to move into property management when the real estate market slowed down. As she sees it, "There may be times when you can't make a sale, and a little income from property management helps pay the rent and keeps you from becoming desperate."

Like so many other successful real estate agents, Lambert is committed to real estate education and says she owes her success to reading, education, and positive thinking. The first African-American woman to hold a certified Real Estate Manager designation from the National Association of Real Estate Brokers, Lambert has also completed many courses in real estate and business management. She now hopes to study appraisal in order to "have a career for my retirement."

Lambert has also been active in community and real estate committees. She was president and chairman of the Dearborn Real Estate Board in 1980–1981 and received the organization's outstanding leadership and service award. In 1974 she was appointed by the Governor of Illinois to serve on the Governor's Commission of Mortgage Practices. Her numerous awards include the "Sanctity of Contract" award from the Intercounty Title Company of Illinois and a certificate for supporting democracy in housing from the Cincinnati Association of Real Estate Boards. Active in African-American causes, Lambert believes there are good opportunities for African-Americans and other minorities in the real estate field. But she also believes that African-American brokers are excluded from many larger and more lucrative land and development projects.

3

PREPARING FOR A REAL ESTATE CAREER

NOW THAT YOU have begun to consider a career in real estate, it is important to determine a course of study that will prepare you to excel at your chosen profession. Unlike many other career choices, there are very few formal education or experience requirements for individuals entering the real estate field. Although all states and the District of Columbia do require real estate agents to pass a proficiency examination before working in the profession, many states do not require very extensive study before taking the test. However, this does not mean that it is not advisable to select and follow a course of study to prepare for a career in the real estate field.

Educational Preparation

High School Diploma

All states require prospective real estate salespeople to hold a high school diploma as a requirement for licensure. Today this is considered the minimum education necessary to engage in the real estate field. Prospective agents who have not completed high school should consider taking the GED equivalency test.

Students interested in a real estate career can begin working toward this goal in high school. Since the real estate field requires both business and mathematical skills and the ability to communicate effectively, a student is advised to take a balanced course of study featuring both English and math. A suggested curriculum would include:

English—3 or 4 years
Math—3 years
Social Sciences—2 years
  (Consider taking psychology.)
History—1 year
  (Students also should consider taking economics, if this course is offered.)

If the student intends to go on to college, he or she should include one or two years of science and one to two years of a foreign language. Other courses that would be beneficial to those considering a real estate career include: public speaking, debate, accounting or bookkeeping, and typing. Needless to say, if your school offers a course in real estate principles, take it. However, few such courses are found at the high school level. Do consider any courses that relate to real estate or finance. For example, many schools offer consumer information courses on home buying, which will provide background on buying and owning a home.

Even high school is not too early to begin working on another important element in the real estate field—public contact. Become active in school and community groups that interest you. Contacts and public visibility are extremely important to success in the real estate field.

Getting a College Degree

Unlike many business fields, real estate does not require a college degree for entrance. However, as we have seen, the trend in real estate is toward a college-educated sales force. In 2000 approximately 87 percent of the salespeople and 90 percent of the brokers in the 2001 National Association of REALTORS (NAR) survey had at least some college background. Although a selling ability is still the important factor in real estate, today's salesperson must be able to deal with complex financial and legal problems. For this reason many firms prefer to hire college graduates who they believe are better able to deal with these new complexities.

If a would-be real estate agent does decide to continue his or her education, the next question becomes what to study. According to the 1999–2000 *Occupational Outlook Handbook*, approximately one thousand schools nationwide offer real estate training. Some offer graduate or undergraduate degrees in real estate, urban land use, construction, or related subjects. Among the courses that are usually found in real estate majors are business and real estate law, accounting, psychology, marketing, management, financial analysis, economics, construction, appraisal, investments, and business communications. More advanced degrees usually put greater emphasis on urban planning and/or financial analysis, while associate degrees often put emphasis on business and marketing skills.

Degree programs in real estate are still a relatively new academic discipline. In the past most real estate courses either have been directed toward urban planners or have been designed primarily to satisfy requirements for licensure. Today more and more schools have expanded and developed real estate departments and professorships. As many real estate departments are located at state-supported schools, real estate instruction is readily available and very affordable to most students. The trend of the future is toward college- and graduate-level real estate education, and those considering real estate careers in the future will need to be better educated than ever to succeed.

College Courses Other Than Real Estate

Although it may be desirable to take courses in real estate, there are many other courses of study that will provide a valuable background for the agent. If the student does not major in real estate, he or she should consider at least a few courses in business and accounting, finance, and economics. As with the high school curriculum, the student is advised to take some courses in English, psychology, Web development, and marketing. Prelaw courses with emphasis on business or property law will help to introduce the agent to the important legal principles inherent in real estate transactions. A course in architecture will give the prospective student some knowledge of housing styles. A course in drafting or architectural drawing will help the student understand housing construction. These suggested courses also would serve as adequate credits toward an undergraduate degree before undertaking graduate work in real estate. However, students should check catalogs carefully for graduate program requirements.

Home Study Courses

Although it is usually not possible to get a degree in real estate through home study, there are quite a few schools that offer one or more courses in real estate for home study. Some of these courses are part of a degree program in business or prelaw, while others are offered for high school credit. (Only some states will accept home study courses to meet licensing requirements.)

Private Real Estate Schools

In addition to colleges and universities, real estate courses are offered by for-profit business schools. These schools usually concentrate on courses that are required by the states to sit for the licensing exam. Few offer any degree program. Though some of these schools provide excellent exam preparation, it is advisable to check carefully before enrolling, since the cost is often higher than comparable courses at a community college. Check to see if the school appears on the list of approved schools issued by the licensing agency of your state. Courses offered by local real estate boards or recognized brokerage firms may give some guarantee of quality.

Licensure

Even if you have completed a degree in real estate, you cannot immediately enter the real estate field. Like many professions from law to barbering, real estate agents must be licensed in the state where they will do business. All states and the District of Columbia require real estate salespeople and brokers to pass a written examination before licensure. In addition many states require applicants to complete some type of real estate course prior to testing, although in some cases those holding college degrees in real estate may be exempted from the requirement.

Because real estate licensure is controlled on the state level, there are variances in requirements. To a great extent these have been lessened through the efforts of the Association of Real Estate License Law Officials (ARELLO), which has worked to establish national standards for licensure. These efforts have made it possible for states to offer reciprocal agreements to each other. A reciprocal agreement between two states permits a broker or agent holding a license in one state to be granted a license in another state without the need to fulfill all of the requirements of the second state.

Because of the differences in state requirements, generalizations are difficult, but there are certain requirements that are widespread. Applicants for a real estate salesperson's license are usually required to be eighteen years old and have a high school diploma. Many states require that the applicant has been a resident of the state for a certain period of time (often six months to one year). Those applying for real estate brokers' licenses must usually meet additional requirements. They must often be twenty-one years old and have been active in the business for a set number of years. Since requirements vary, check with the licensing agency in your state to be certain that you have satisfied all requirements.

Educational Requirements

In addition to age and experience requirements, the majority of states require prospective real estate agents to complete some type of course in real estate principles and practices at a real estate school accredited by the state. Many states require real estate salespeople to complete a course of between thirty and ninety classroom hours of instruction. These courses will cover the basic laws governing the ownership and transfer of real estate. Students will be taught to understand the terms of sales contracts and other documents commonly used in real estate transactions and learn how to fill them out. Students also will be taught the regulations that control the real estate business in their state. Students will learn how mortgages work and the advantages and disadvantages of different types of financing. They will receive instructions in the provisions of the federal fair housing law and other federal and state laws that guarantee equal rights and protect consumers.

Applicants for a broker's license must usually take more complex courses than those required for salespeople. Courses may range from 20 to 120 additional hours of study. Brokers will cover the finer points of real property law and contract law and study the responsibilities of the broker toward his or her clients and to the salespeople under his or her supervision. In addition brokers' courses are often taught on special aspects of real estate such as property management, finance, and appraisal. Some other courses address business and management topics.

In general the trend in real estate licensure is toward more extensive educational requirements. In the past few years many states have increased educational requirements for both salespeople and brokers. This trend toward higher education is also reflected in the growing number of states that require some agents to take a specified number of courses to retain a real estate license. As of 2000, all but one state required some amount of continuing education to keep a real estate license active. Requirements ranged from twelve to seventy hours of class work every two years. Check with your state licensing agency to find out about its continuing education requirement.

Licensing Examinations

Whether or not the prospective real estate agent has to take a real estate course, all states require that he or she pass a written examination to obtain a license. These tests are usually one-day examinations given monthly or bimonthly at various locations throughout the state. Most state exams are divided into two parts—general real estate questions and state-specific questions. The general, or uniform, questions section is always the longest, usually ranging in length from 100 to 150 questions. The questions in the uniform part of the exam cover topics such as:

1. Real estate contracts—the meaning of various clauses within a specific contract, the legal obligations of contracts, and the elements of that contract. Some state examinations will require the student to complete a real estate sales contract using supplied information.
2. Real estate brokerage—the understanding of various functions and responsibilities of the real estate agent and the agent's legal obligations to the client.
3. Real estate financing—the types of mortgages available for real estate and the legal obligations of the buyer.
4. Real estate ownership laws—the elements of a deed and different types of deeds, different ownership rights in land and the attributes of each, and the fair housing law and any other consumer rights laws.
5. Real estate valuation—how to evaluate property and how real estate taxes are determined.

The uniform brokers' examination covers most of the same topics in greater detail. In addition, brokers will be expected to answer questions on:

1. the broker's responsibility to customers and salespeople
2. leasing and portions of a lease
3. real estate investment procedures
4. closing procedures and computations

The state-specific portion of the examination is separate from the uniform portion and usually consists of between 20 and 50 questions concerned with real estate procedures particular to that state. Students will be questioned on the state license law, state consumer legislation, and any other real estate laws that are not common national practice.

Most real estate examinations are made up of short-answer questions that require the student to recall facts and make judgments based on knowledge. Most examinations include a certain number of questions that require the examinee to do simple mathematical calculations. Some states permit the use of calculators; check with the state examining agency before taking the test.

Many states use standardized tests prepared by an outside testing company such as Assessment Systems, Inc., Balacynwyd, Pennsylvania; and Applied Measurement Professionals, Lenexa, Kansas. These tests are similar in format to college entrance examination tests you may have taken in the past. They use machine graded score sheets; the student fills in the space under the correct answer. In some cases the testing service provides only the uniform portion of the examination, and the state section is prepared by a state group. Still other states use a test prepared by Assessment Systems, Inc. called the Real Estate Assessment for Licensure (REAL) program.

When you apply to take a state exam, the licensing agency will usually send a booklet explaining the testing procedure and the types of questions that will be asked. Although each state exam is different, the following will give you some indication of the types of questions that appear on licensing exams:

1. Michele Harper owns a parcel of land. Jack Ryan takes possession of the land after obtaining Harper's permission. Ryan's possession continues for fifteen years. Ryan then tries to get a legal title to the property. Will he succeed?
   A. Ryan will be successful because he lived on the property for fifteen years without interruption.
   B. Ryan will be successful because he satisfied all the requirements for eminent domain.
   C. Ryan will not be successful because he cannot obtain title to the property just by living on it for a certain number of years.
   D. Ryan will not be successful because not all the requirements for adverse possession have been met.

   The answer here is D.

2. Frank Lane wants to know how much money he still owes on his mortgage. He knows that the interest portion of the last monthly payment was $291.42. If he pays 8 1/4 percent interest on the loan, what is his outstanding balance?
   A. $43,713.00
   B. $42,388.36
   C. $36,427.50
   D. $34,284.70

   The correct answer is B.

3. The rights of a surviving husband in the real estate owned by a deceased spouse during their marriage are called:
   A. Dower
   B. Curtesy

C. Homestead
D. Escheat

The correct answer is B.

Each state sets its own passing scores for the examination, with most states requiring examinees to have a score of between seventy and seventy-five to pass. In general, students may retake the examination as many times as necessary to pass. Some states do require applicants to wait for a short period before retaking the test, if the applicant has failed twice.

Receiving a License

If the prospective applicant has passed the examination and met all of the other state requirements for licensure, the state real estate commission will issue a license to the applicant. All states require new agents to pay a licensing fee of from $25 to $150. Since salespeople must be associated with a broker, persons applying for a salesperson's license must submit the name of the broker with whom they will be associated before the commission will issue a license. The broker who "holds" a salesperson's license is legally responsible for the actions of the salesperson, and the salesperson can receive a license only *after* he or she has become associated with a broker.

Other Education for Real Estate Agents

Although the real estate agent must meet only state requirements to obtain a license, additional education is available to those already in the field as well as to those who are training for the business. Many associations and national real estate franchises offer training via the

Internet. One option is through the NAR at realtoruniversity.com. Try also realestate.university.com.

The National Association of REALTORS and other real estate associations also offer numerous courses and books to help real estate professionals. Many courses are taught through state and local NAR chapters, called *boards*. Perhaps the first course suitable for the needs of the new real estate agent is the Graduate, Realtors Institute (GRI) course. This course is made up of several courses, which are usually offered in sequence and cover such topics as real estate law, finance, appraisal, office management, and selling techniques. After completing the courses, the student earns the GRI designation.

Other real estate organizations also offer courses. The Appraisal Institute offers two designations that are available for students who have met certain education and experience requirements. The Member, Appraisal Institute (MAI) designation has higher requirements as to experience and education in all forms of real estate appraisal. To receive an MAI, an applicant must hold a college degree or comply with special requirements; have five years of appraisal experience, three of which must be in specialized appraisal; pass several examinations; and pass a demonstration report. To maintain the designation, members must complete continuing education requirements.

The Appraisal Institute also offers the SRA designation for Specialist, Residential Appraisal. Many of the qualifications are parallel to the MAI, but a college degree is not required.

In the special area of managing residential and commercial real estate, the Institute of Real Estate Management (IREM) offers several designations. The Certified Property Manager (CPM) designation requires applicants to have from three to five years' experience in property management and to complete several courses on such subjects as managing personnel, developing budgeting and accounting procedures, maintaining the building, and understanding legal requirements of leasing. In addition to basic management skills, specialized courses are conducted in managing apartment buildings, condominiums, office buildings, public housing projects, commercial buildings, and shopping centers. The Accredited Residential Manager (ARM) designation requires the applicant to take a basic course in residential management to qualify for the accreditation.

Most of the other NAR associations offer one or more courses leading to a specialty designation. The American Society of Real Estate Counselors offers a Counselor of Real Estate (CRE) designation, and the Society of Office and Industrial Realtors also conducts courses leading to professional designations. The REALTORS have specialized councils that offer courses leading to several designations, including Certified Residential Specialist and Certified Residential Brokerage Manager. The Commercial-Investment Real Estate Institute (CIREI) awards the Certified Commercial-Investment Member designation to qualified commercial brokers.

In addition to designations courses, both the NAR and its affiliates as well as other real estate organizations, sponsor courses and seminars on topics of interest to its members. State and local real estate boards also offer courses that help real estate agents increase their knowledge and skills. The Institute of Real Estate Management, the Appraisal Institute, the Commercial-Investment Real Estate Institute, and other associations also publish textbooks, journals, and newsletters for their members, such as the IREM's *Journal of Property Management* and CCIM Institute's *Commercial Investment Journal.* These publications keep agents informed about new developments in their fields and provide them with a forum for the discussion of real estate issues.

Other public and private organizations also offer real estate courses. Most of the courses offered by community colleges are designed for those preparing for the licensing examination, but most institutions will admit students on a part-time basis. Another source of education, particularly on selling skills, are independent seminars offered by individuals or firms. There are numerous for-profit schools and individuals conducting courses to help salespeople increase their selling and business skills. Although there are many selling techniques that can be of benefit to prospective real estate agents, the student should be careful to check the credentials of the instructor before enrolling in the often expensive courses. Courses in selling skills, brokerage techniques, and other topics are also offered by many real estate firms. These courses can be of great benefit in increasing your skills, and you should consider the educational program of a firm when you select a prospective employer.

Because real estate is a topic of such interest to everyone, many publishers are issuing books on real estate sales and investment. Although some of these books are intended for consumers, they will give the student some information on real estate transactions and the current issues in real estate. Other books focus on other skills. (See Appendix C for a partial list of books on real estate topics.)

Experience Opportunities

Because you need a license to sell real estate, it is difficult to get any job experience before you complete the necessary education.

However, there are still some options open to those who want exposure to the field. All real estate offices employ clerical personnel to answer the telephone and handle routine office work. These people are not allowed by law to conduct any real estate business, but the attentive worker will learn a great deal about the real estate business through observation.

A middle ground for gaining real estate experience without plunging directly into sales is by becoming a real estate personal assistant. According to the *1999 NAR Profile of Real Estate Firms*, 39 percent of firms employ personal assistants. Depending on the duties they perform and the laws in their state, assistants may or may not hold a real estate license. But in many cases, they perform at least some administrative duties and receive a regular salary from their employer. They also may receive bonuses or commissions if they take part in actual selling activities.

If you are already employed in another field, the best way to acquire real estate experience might be to secure a license and try to work in real estate on a part-time basis. This will give you the chance to learn about the business without sacrificing your current position, although part-time work is less available than it once was. You can also gain valuable experience in the field by working in an area closely allied to real estate such as banking, construction, finance, or law. Working in any related field can help you to understand certain aspects of the real estate business and give you that much more knowledge when you do decide to enter real estate.

Another way of preparing for the real estate business is to begin acquiring a good working knowledge of the community in which you live. This will be invaluable to you when you begin your real estate career, since much of the success of a real estate agent rests on his or her familiarity with the community. Learn the location of schools, shopping centers, and recreational areas in your community. Join the civic and social groups that interest you. Read the real estate and business sections of your local paper to increase your understanding of the real estate market in your area and to learn about new real estate developments. These organizations not only will enrich your life but will provide you with valuable sources of clients once you begin your career. Find out about laws such as zoning regulations and housing codes in your area. These can affect the price and construction of houses. Like almost any other field, there are many sources of information that are open to the student who is willing to investigate. By doing research the prospective real estate agent can find enough information to decide whether his or her interests and abilities match the demands of the field.

4

How to Select a Company

Once you have obtained the necessary education to enter the real estate field, you need to select a real estate firm to hold your license. All licensed real estate salespeople must be associated with a broker in order to be active in the real estate field. In choosing a brokerage office, there are a great many factors to consider. In this chapter we will try to cover some of them. Remember, however, that location should have a tremendous influence on the "right" firm. A firm with national recognition may not be as important in a small town, and a franchise may not be as attractive if it has strong independent competition. A large firm with many offices or departments may offer more resources and more opportunities to try different specialties or to advance on the corporate ladder. Do careful research in your area to find the best firm there.

Training

Perhaps the most important factor to consider in selecting a real estate office is the amount of training and support the firm can provide for its salespeople. This is especially true for those who are entering real estate for the first time. Although some education is required before you can begin practicing real estate, many real estate agents have had very little experience in the day-to-day activities of the brokerage office. It is important to find a firm that will offer education, training, and experience in selling and listing skills and other tasks that the salesperson will be called on to perform. Training courses may also provide exposure to areas of real estate that were not covered in the salesperson's prelicensing training. These may include more advanced topics such as appraisal and financing. Many firms run in-house programs for their salespeople. These may vary from informal courses run by a broker to regular classes conducted by a sales or training manager. The prospective salesperson should check to see how often the sessions are offered and if there are any set topics that are covered regularly. It is also wise to ask if the courses are offered to the firm's salespeople free of charge.

Because most salespeople work as independent contractors, the firm does not usually reimburse the agent for courses taken outside the firm. However, the salesperson should consider the firm's attitude to education in making his or her selection. Does the firm encourage its salespeople to take courses and post notices of available courses in the area? Ask the broker how many salespeople have completed a course in the last year.

Becoming a member of associations such as the National Association of REALTORS (NAR) also gives salespeople access to courses and online information created just for members. For example, NAR offers members online business tools on the Web at realtormag.com and free access to a large library of real estate–related publications at onerealtorplace.com.

Another type of training that will be of benefit to the new salesperson is working with an experienced salesperson. Even with classroom work, the new agent may not encounter all of the situations that can come up in everyday business. For this reason, working in tandem with a seasoned agent will teach the new salesperson techniques that might not be covered in class. Ask the broker if this type of support is available with the firm.

One of the factors that can influence a salesperson's success is the success of his or her firm. What is the firm's reputation in the community? Ask local business leaders, lawyers, and the Better Business Bureau about the firm's background. In investigating a possible brokerage, try to get a picture of where the firm is situated in relation to its competitors. Compare the average sales price of the firm's houses to those of others in the community. A firm in the same area as several other successful and aggressive businesses may be having difficulty retaining its share of the clients. Ask what percentage of the market the firm currently holds. Also get information on the growth of the firm over the last few years. Good indications of growth include an increase in the number of sales associates, the opening of a new office, or an increase in the number of support employees. Obviously a firm that has had a steady growth offers greater stability and opportunity than a firm that is just barely making it. It is also important to talk with the broker and find out the firm's projections for growth in the future. In asking questions about the firm's growth, the prospective salesperson should also find out about the possibilities for advancement and management training that the firm can promise.

Services and Facilities

The real estate agent should also study the services and benefits offered by the firm. Review the firm's advertising program and see how often the advertising appears. Look at the ads themselves to see what qualities and image the firm projects. You should also consider the effectiveness of the advertising.

Since support staff is extremely important to the performance of real estate jobs, be certain that sufficient office support is provided to salespeople. Also determine what jobs the secretaries are expected to perform. Check the number of secretaries in relation to the number of salespeople. If there are too few secretaries, they will find it difficult to complete all of the work, especially during peak periods. Many successful real estate agents hire their own assistants to handle follow-up work.

Consider the location of the firm's office. If the office is located in the middle of a prosperous shopping or business district, it is more likely to be well known to customers. Such a firm is also likely to receive a certain amount of business from people who just walk into the firm without any prior knowledge of its background. Some brokers are also interested in finding offices that are located close to their homes. This can have the obvious advantage of making the trip to and from work easier. In addition it may be of benefit to the agent because he or she is more likely to know the area near the firm and its potential clients. This knowledge of an area is one of the assets that a real estate agent brings to the profession.

It is also important to consider the physical layout and look of the office. Does the office present an attractive appearance to potential clients? Be sure that there are enough desks, telephones, and other equipment for all of the salespeople associated with the firm. Is the other equipment such as copy machines and computers up-to-date and in good working order? Today computerized listings of properties for sale are a major source of sales for most real estate agents. Not only is this equipment necessary for the salesperson to do his or her job, its condition may be an indication of the professionalism and financial condition of the firm. The size, design, and sophistication of the company's Web page is another good indicator of a firm's growth potential. Ask the broker how many leads are generated from the company's site. While you are investigating the office, also look at the stationery, "for sale" signs, and other written materials of the office to see that they are attractive and in good supply.

Another clue to the prosperity of the office may be gained by looking at the salespeople. Look at their clothes and the age and appearance of their cars. This may be some indication of their incomes and that of the company. The appearance of the salespeople associated with the firm will also contribute to the general appearance and atmosphere of the firm. When investigating the salespeople, a new salesperson should also consider the personalities of the other associates. Although this may not have a major impact on the selling ability of the other agents, a wise person will try to select a firm where the salespeople are congenial with his or her personality. As in any other job, the people with whom you work have a major impact on how you feel about your job. Finding an office where you feel at home is as important as finding one where you can make the most money.

How do the firm's salespeople feel about the firm? Try to find what the turnover rate is in the office; that is, how many people leave the firm for other jobs in a year's period. See how the associates feel about the firm. Try to visit the firm when some of the salespeople are in the office. Ask if you can talk with them and try to see what they say about the firm. Even though there will always be those who complain or praise too much, you still might get an idea of how the salespeople feel about their firm.

Earning Potential

Of course one of the most important questions to ask in considering a new firm is what kind of commission rates it pays. Although commission rates are always worked out on an individual basis between the broker and the salesperson, most firms in an area offer comparable commission rates, with between 6 and 7 percent of the sale price as the norm. In general the salesperson who makes the sale receives approximately 40 to 50 percent of this overall commission, which is then shared with his or her firm. The remaining commission is divided between the firm the selling broker works for and the salesperson who obtained the listing on the property. In many cases brokers have agreements with some salespeople to pay a higher percentage of the commission once they have made a certain amount in any year. Commission rates for salespeople who receive a salary as well as a commission receive a lesser commission rate, usually about 25 percent of the overall commission.

The Size of the Firm

If the benefits and facilities a firm has to offer are similar, the salesperson should next decide whether he or she wants to work for a large or small firm. There are obviously advantages and disadvantages to each of these alternatives. The majority of firms in the United States have ten or fewer sales associates. In fact the *1999 NAR Profile of Real Estate Firms* found that 60 percent of all firms had five or fewer sales associates. However, firms with more than fifty employees employ 38 percent of all sales associates. Mergers and consolidations are also increasing the number of larger firms. Though the majority of these smaller firms are located in less populated areas, you will still find many smaller firms in large urban areas.

Many beginning agents believe that a small firm can provide them with more personal guidance as they begin their careers. This may be true, but larger firms and firms associated with franchising organizations are more likely to provide formal in-house training programs than smaller independent offices. Another advantage of larger offices is that they usually have larger advertising budgets than do smaller firms. This will make it more likely for customers to be acquainted with the firm. In addition larger firms are more likely to have administrators, sales managers, and other managers who can instruct the salesperson in specialized areas. On the other hand, the practices of a large firm may not be suited to those real estate brokers who are interested in opening their own businesses. By working in a small office you can gain firsthand experience in operating a small business. Even though the size of the office may have some impact on the nature of the business, a small firm can offer as many opportunities to the new broker as the larger firm.

A continuing trend in real estate is the increased centralization and consolidation of the industry. Many real estate firms are seeking to achieve regional or even national dominance by acquiring other firms. Twelve percent of all firms opened an additional office in 1999, according to the *1999 NAR Profile of Real Estate Firms.*

Insurance companies, REITs (real estate investment trusts), real estate operating companies, and some banks also own, sell, and manage large portfolios of real estate. Some analysts predict that real estate giants will soon control the majority of the market.

The national or large regional real estate company may have a more formal business environment than the small independent office. But it is also likely to offer more training and other benefits than the local firm. In addition, the national firm offers the ambitious agent much greater opportunities for advancement than an owner-held office. Because large firms employ more administrators than smaller firms, there are more management positions available in them than there are in the smaller firms. In addition, just as the larger local firm has more than one office where the salesperson can work, the consolidated firm may have offices nationwide. These advantages make larger firms particularly attractive to college-educated agents interested in moving into management.

The Firm's Affiliations

As important as the firm's size is its business affiliations. In selecting a firm, the agent should find out whether the broker is a member of the National Association of REALTORS or other trade association. Although there are some fine firms that are not REALTOR members, the association does provide educational materials, information on the state of the real estate business, and other facts that might be helpful to the active agent. Many local boards also offer multiple listing services that can benefit local firms.

Another affiliation that may be of use to a firm is its membership in a franchise. Franchise operations are national networks of individually owned brokerage firms, all of which use the trade name and basic operating procedures of the parent franchise. Some of the most common real estate franchises are Century 21, ERA, RE/MAX, and Coldwell Banker.

Most franchises offer other benefits to their members, such as training material and administrative guidelines. They often give their members assistance in accounting, financing, and office procedures. Franchises also advertise on a national level, thus giving their members customer identification.

Brokerage firms of all sizes belong to franchises, although for some reason larger and smaller firms are more likely to be franchise members than mid-size firms. Even though franchise fees are often high, most brokers who are members believe that overall the franchise has increased their business.

The power of franchises has remained fairly steady. In 1992, 24 percent of firms and 42 percent of the sales force were affiliated with franchised agencies, according to an NAR survey. By 1999, 22 percent of firms and 38 percent of the sales force were represented by franchises.

Going into Business for Yourself

Although the salesperson who is just entering the real estate field should not consider going into his or her own business, many salespeople and brokers have this goal in the backs of their minds. Approximately 26 percent of the real estate brokers questioned in the NAR survey owned their own firms while another 20 percent had some ownership interest in the firm for which they worked.

The decision to go into business for yourself is a complex one. Many good salespeople do not make good managers. The average broker who owns his or her own firm can generally earn more in a year than one who does not, but the owner-broker is certain to have more administrative responsibilities than the salesperson. And since most smaller offices do not produce enough income to hire a full-time manager, the broker will have to perform managerial duties in addition to whatever selling he or she does.

As for any small business, the risk of failure for a brokerage firm is high. Many new brokers do not have enough business experience to handle the business. In addition many brokers try to open new firms without sufficient capital. A new broker must establish a presentable office in a desirable location. The cost of maintaining a real estate office may be less than for some other businesses, but it is still expensive to buy office furnishings; pay for stationery, signs, and cards; and pay rent, telephone, and utility bills. The new broker also must do some initial advertising to inform the public about the firm's opening. It is a rule of thumb that new businesses should have enough capital to keep their doors open for at least six months before they expect to make a profit, so this capital should include not only the money needed to open the office but whatever monies are needed to keep it running until commissions begin to come in. The new broker should also have enough in reserve to cover his or her living expenses. These expenses have to be paid whether or not a sale is made! In addition, because there is often a lapse of from thirty to ninety days between the time the sale is made and commission is collected, the new owner will have to consider this in his or her income calculations.

With that said, once established a real estate firm often stays in business for many years. According to the *1999 NAR Profile of Real Estate Firms*, a typical brokerage firm has been in the business for thirteen years. Approximately 30 percent of all firms had been in business for more than twenty-five years.

How Long Does It Take to Get Started?

Once you have selected a real estate office, do not expect to make a sale immediately. As we have indicated, even the salesperson who has done well in his or her education may have a great deal to learn about selling and the day-to-day operations of a real estate office. Becoming familiar with the contracts, financing options, and listing techniques may take some time. In addition it may be hard at first to find clients. Even family and friends may be reluctant to give their real estate business to an inexperienced salesperson. Finally, even if you do make a sale in the first week, it may take from a month to three months to collect the commission. In addition, about 5 percent of all transactions are not completed for one reason or another. These failed sales produce no income at all.

As in all other professions, success in real estate does not come in a day or a week. But it can come to those who have an interest in the field and who are willing to work hard in acquiring and practicing real estate skills.

5

THE REAL ESTATE AGENT'S JOB

IN THE PRECEDING chapters we discussed the real estate industry and its opportunities. In this chapter we will focus on what the real estate broker or salesperson really does. Because the vast majority of those working in this field are primarily involved in residential sales, this chapter will focus on the activities of residential sales agents. Chapter 6 will explore the jobs of commercial sales, appraisal, development, and other real estate specialties.

Even within the area of residential sales, however, the real estate agent carries out numerous activities to sell even one piece of property. Residential brokers and salespeople do much more than just show houses to prospective buyers. Agents obtain listings from people interested in selling their homes. They work with the buyer and the seller to arrive at a sales agreement. They assist the buyers in locating adequate financing, and they help to conduct the closing of the sale and arrange for the actual transfer of the property. Every one of these activities and more must be carried out before the agent can collect the commission on even one sale.

Listing the Property

In the real estate agent's job, getting a listing for a property is just as important as selling it. A listing is an agreement between a home owner and a real estate firm that the firm will act on behalf of the owner to try and find buyers for the property. In obtaining a listing, the real estate salesperson is acquiring the product that he or she will sell to the public. A real estate broker who does not obtain good listings is unlikely to have much success, regardless of his or her selling skills. So important are listings that the listing agent receives a part of the commission when the property is sold. Because listings are such an important element of the real estate business, agents usually spend a portion of every business day in acquiring new listings.

Listings can come from a variety of sources. The traditional method of obtaining new listings is through blind solicitations. The real estate agent designates a specific geographical area, sometimes called a *farm* in real estate slang. He or she then either telephones or visits residents in the area to find out whether they are interested in selling their homes. Obviously this method assumes a high failure rate. However, even if an owner is not now interested in selling, the agent can establish a contact that may pay off in business at some later date.

There are many other methods used by real estate brokers to secure listings. An agent can study local newspapers for news of new arrivals, recent promotions, marriages, new children, divorces, or deaths of spouses. Each of these events may produce the need to buy or sell a home and provide the agent with a new client. Once the agent has been in the real estate business for a number of years, referrals from past clients also will provide a source of new listings. Satisfied clients will be very likely to think of a particular firm if they need real estate services later. Most real estate agents devote some time to maintaining contact with former clients. They may call customers at yearly intervals to discuss possible real estate needs. Many agents use mailings at Christmas, anniversaries of home purchase, or other occasions to keep in touch with former clients. New agents can send mailings to friends and former business associates informing them of the agent's entry into the real estate business. Some agencies even send regular newsletters to local residents and former clients.

One of the major sources of listings for many firms is the multiple listing service. A multiple listing service is a central clearinghouse for all listings obtained by the cooperating firms, and it is available both online and in print form. All of the information about listings is made available to all of the firms in the service. Any firm in the service may then try to find a buyer for the property. If a firm does make a sale, a portion of the commission is paid to the firm that obtained the listing. Multiple listing services are often operated by local real estate boards affiliated with the National Association of REALTORS (NAR). Today multiple listing services are computerized.

Many prospective buyers will come to a real estate firm in response to advertisements of "for sale" signs. However, aggressive salespeople will be able to find prospective buyers from many of the areas discussed above. In general the more people an agent knows in the community and the more he or she participates in community activities, the more likely it is that people looking for a home will think of the agent's firm. Some real estate firms are even listing their properties on the World Wide Web.

Once the real estate salesperson has established contact with a person who is interested in selling his or her home, the agent must convince the seller that the firm the agent represents will provide the services that the seller needs. To a great extent the agent is selling his or her expertise and the expertise of his or her firm. Sellers do not have to use the services of a real estate firm; they can simply run their own advertisement and look for buyers. Since the seller is responsible for paying the commission to the real estate firm, many sellers think that they can save money by selling the property themselves. It is the job of the real estate agent to convince the seller that the services of his or her real estate firm will guarantee the seller a faster, less troublesome, and more profitable sale. In soliciting listings, agents will usually emphasize the number and experience of the firm's sales force, the success of past sales, and the extent of the firm's advertising. Many firms provide salespeople with listing presentation books containing background information on the firm, examples of the firm's advertising, and sample contracts. Agents also will emphasize their expertise in securing the necessary financing, negotiating contracts, and handling the details of the sale. Finally agents usually point out the time and trouble involved in showing property.

The Listing Agreement

Once an agreement is reached between the seller and the real estate agent, they will sign a listing agreement setting out the terms of the relationship. Listing agreements usually specify the rate of commission and the amount that the seller wants for the property and give specifics about the house, such as the number of bathrooms, type of heating, and what items are included in the sale. Listing agreements are usually made for a term of 90 to 120 days and may or may not give the right to sell exclusively to the one firm.

One of the most difficult parts of drawing up the listing contract is agreeing on a price for the property. It is usually the responsibility of the sellers to tell the broker what price they want for the house. However, most sellers do not know housing prices in their area. In addition they often have an emotional attachment to the home that may lead them to overvalue it. Before making the listing presentation, the salesperson should check recent sales prices of other comparable homes in the area to get some idea of what price the house will bring. He or she also should make note of how these other homes compare in features with the home being listed. By letting the sellers know what other houses sold for, the salesperson can help them to arrive at a price that will satisfy them and will still be reasonable. An overpriced home probably will not sell, leaving unsatisfied sellers and no commission.

The Buyer's Agent

Traditionally, most residential sales agents have represented the seller in the real estate transaction; today, some agents specialize in representing the buyer. According to the 2000 NAR *Profile of Home Buyers and Home Sellers*, 15 percent of all home buyers used a buyer's agent. Buyers' representatives help buyers locate appropriate homes, help them evaluate the homes they see, assist in locating and arranging financing, and represent the buyers in all negotiations. Buyers' representatives have contracts of employment with the buyers and are either paid directly by them or receive a portion of the sales commission from the listing broker. Because many of the skills needed to be a buyer's agent are similar to those for any real estate salesperson, the Real Estate Buyer's Agent Council offers the designation Accredited Buyer

Representative (ABR) to those who have completed special courses on servicing buyers.

Selling the Property

Getting Ready

The next major task of the real estate broker is to show the property to prospective buyers. Before showing the property, the agent should spend time going over the house to learn about the features that will appeal to buyers. The house's architecture, landscaping, and location will all be important selling points. Luxury features such as greenhouses, fireplaces, and swimming pools will appeal to some buyers. Agents should be aware of schools, shopping facilities, and transportation in the area so that out-of-town buyers can appreciate the advantages of the location. The agent should check on the zoning laws, tax rates, and other regulations that may affect the value of the property. The agent also will want to go over the home with the seller to see if there are any improvements, such as repainting, that should be done before the property is shown to buyers.

The next job of the agent is to inform the public and other real estate firms about the availability of the property. Often the first step in informing the public of a house's availability is with a "for sale" sign. An attractive sign showing the name of the firm and the agent is an effective and inexpensive way to reach the buying public. Agents usually duplicate information about the property and distribute it to other agents in the firm and, if applicable, to the multiple listing service.

Real estate agents also will discuss with their brokers the amount of advertising that will be done for the property. Policies for advertising an individual home differ from firm to firm. Because of the cost of advertising, most firms will use only classified ads when advertising an individual property. In other cases the firm may run a larger display advertisement with pictures that highlight several of the firm's properties. If the firm is selling houses in a new development or units in a condominium, the firm may decide to advertise just that group of homes.

Open Houses

Another method used by real estate agents to sell property is conducting an open house. At an open house, the house is available for viewing at any time during a set period. In preparing for an open house, the agent will have to work out a suitable time with the seller. Then he or she will have to place signs advertising the open house on roads leading to the property. The agent may also discuss with his or her broker the possibility of running special advertising to tie in with the open house. On the day of the open house, the agent will be responsible for ensuring that there is at least one agent on the premises during the entire period of the open house. The advantages of a successful open house for the agent is that more prospective buyers can view the property during a shorter period.

Showing the Property

One of the most important skills that a real estate agent must learn is how to show a property effectively. This really requires two separate skills: knowing the features of the property and understanding the wants and needs of the buyers. We have already discussed that the agent should familiarize himself or herself with each property before beginning to show it. It is equally important to learn what the buyers are looking for in a new home. Salespeople should determine the size and features of the home the buyers need and how much they will be able to pay. In addition the agent should decide what amenities the buyers want. Is a beautiful yard more important to them than being close to the shopping center? Do they prefer colonial columns or modern glass and steel? In part these questions can be answered by a careful interview before showing even one house. The real estate agent also must learn to be a good judge of people and pay attention to their clothes, personalities, and comments to understand what they are likely to want. Stanford University researchers have determined that about 85 percent of the decision to buy a home is emotional rather than rational. Many buyers may try to be practical in buying a home, but ultimately the decision will be made because of a buyer's basic wants. The smart real estate broker is one who recognizes the importance of these wants and helps the buyer to fulfill them. If an agent has a good understanding of a buyer's needs, he or she can make the job of showing property much easier.

An understanding of prospective buyers' personalities also will help the agent in deciding what selling techniques will be most successful. Some buyers may prefer to have the agent constantly on hand for questions, while others may prefer to wander alone over the property.

Qualifying the Buyer

Once prospective buyers have expressed an interest in a property, the real estate agent should try to determine whether the buyers can afford to buy the property. Before showing the property, the agent will ask the buyers what price range of houses they want. For many years the rule of thumb for real estate sales was that a person could afford to spend 33 percent of his or her income for housing. However, rising housing prices and two-income families have greatly altered the easy rules. In considering whether a person will be able to afford a specific house, the salesperson should take into account the income of the spouse. The agent should also ask about other sources of income, savings accounts, and other assets. In determining how much of a loan the buyer might qualify for, the agent should ask about current debts such as car loans and past credit history. A person with many outstanding bills may not qualify for a loan even if he or she has a large income.

Another factor that will influence the chances of getting a loan is the size of the down payment the buyer plans to make. Usual practice calls for a down payment of between 10 and 20 percent of the sales price. But if a buyer can make a larger initial payment or purchase private mortgage insurance, he or she may be more likely to qualify for a loan.

Another aspect of qualifying a buyer is to help him or her understand the total expenses involved in home ownership. While housing prices themselves have climbed sharply, so too have other costs associated with them. These include rising real estate taxes and home owners insurance, which is required by mortgage lenders. Single family home owners also should include some type of reserve for future maintenance and repairs. And for those buying condominiums, monthly maintenance fees should be included in the cost estimates.

It may not be necessary to do extensive calculations of the buyers' income and liabilities, but the wise salesperson will try to be fairly certain that the buyer can afford the house and qualify for a loan before he or she presents the offer to the sellers. If a sales contract that has been agreed upon by the parties later falls through, the sellers are likely to blame the salesperson and lose confidence in his or her abilities.

Negotiating the Sale

All of the work of showing the property leads up to the job of negotiating the sale. The real estate broker and his or her sales-people are almost always the agents of the sellers and therefore must consider their interests before all others. However, only by helping satisfy the needs of both the buyer and the seller can the agent hope to reach an agreement. Here again it is important to understand the personalities of the parties involved and to select the right techniques for persuading both parties of the advantages of the sale. A reputable salesperson should never use high-pressure tactics, but it is important to get both parties to see the transaction objectively. For many buyers the purchase of a home is a frightening responsibility, and they may hesitate to commit themselves. Sellers may allow their emotional attachment to their home to hinder their willingness to negotiate a price. In presenting an offer to a seller, the salesperson should emphasize the buyer's enthusiasm for the home and the benefits of the proposed agreement to the seller.

Once the terms of the sale have been set, the broker may prepare a sales contract setting out the terms for the sale for both parties to sign. Agents are generally permitted to complete preprinted contracts. However, real estate personnel should be careful not to give legal advice and should urge the parties to consult an attorney if any questions arise. All state laws prohibit brokers from giving legal advice to clients. After signing the sales contract, the buyer will usually deposit a small percentage of the purchase price—called the earnest money deposit—to show that the buyer is "in earnest" about buying the property with the broker. The agent will keep the money in a trust account until the sale is final and then turn it over to the seller. If the buyer defaults on the contract, the seller is usually permitted to keep the deposit. (See sample real estate sale contract.)

Arranging Financing

Many sales contracts include a clause that makes the contract binding only if the buyer is able to find financing to help pay for the property. The price of the median home was approximately $139,000 at the end of 2000, well beyond the means of most people to pay for without borrowing money. Most real estate is financed with mortgages. A mortgage is a contract between the borrower and the lender, usually a savings and loan, under which the borrower agrees to repay the borrowed amount over a certain period. The lender charges a certain percentage of the loan amount as interest, that is, a charge for loaning the money. Most mortgages today are drawn up so that the borrower pays the loan and interest in equal monthly payments over a period of twenty-five or thirty years. Some people choose shorter fifteen-year mortgages to pay off loans more rapidly. In the past, mortgage rates have been set for the entire term of the loan. However, the high interest rates of a few years ago prompted many lenders to introduce adjustable interest rates that move up and down with the inflation rates and protect the lenders in the event inflation continues for some time.

Sample Real Estate Sale Contract

THIS MEMORANDUM WITNESSETH, THAT seller, Angela and Max Hill

hereby agrees to SELL, and purchaser, S. Green

agrees to PURCHASE, at the price of $350,000 (three hundred fifty thousand dollars)

Dollars, the following described real estate, situated in Cook County, Illinois:

1308 North Seneca Street described as Lot #14, Rolling Hills, a subdivision as shown by the recorded plat thereof, City of Skokie, Cook County, Illinois

Subject to (1) existing leases, expiring
the purchaser to be entitled to the rents, if any, from the time of delivery of Deed; (2) all taxes and assessments levied after the year 2001; (3) any unpaid special taxes or assessments, levied for improvements not yet made; also subject to:

Any repairs to the roof considered necessary by a professional inspection.

Purchaser has paid $24,500 (twenty-four thousand five hundred dollars)   Dollars, as earnest money, to be applied on said purchase when consummated, and agrees to pay, within five days after the title has been examined and found good, the further sum of $75,500 (seventy-five thousand five hundred dollars) Dollars, to Lake Title and Trust Company, provided a good and sufficient   recordable Warranty Deed, conveying to purchaser a good title to said premises with waiver and conveyance of any and all estates of homestead therein and all rights of dower, inchoate or otherwise, (subject as aforesaid), shall then be ready for delivery. The balance to be paid as follows:

The buyer being able to obtain a first mortgage in the amount of $250,000 for the term of 30 years.

with interest   at the rate of 6.75   percent per annum, payable semi-annually, to be secured by notes and mortgage, or trust deed, of even date herewith, on said premises, in the form   . Seller shall furnish within a reasonable time a certificate of title issued by the Registrar of Titles of Cook   County or a complete merchantable abstract of title, or a merchantable copy, brought down to date, or a merchantable title insurance policy (or commitment) of   brought down to date. In case the title upon examination is found materially defective, within ten days after said abstract, certificate of title or title insurance policy (or commitment) is furnished, then, unless the material defects be cured within sixty days after written notice thereof, the said earnest money shall be refunded and this contract is to be inoperative.

   Seller warrants to purchaser that no notice from any city, village or other governmental authority of a dwelling code violation which existed in the dwelling structure before the execution of this contract has been received by the seller, his principal or his agent within 10 years of the date of execution of this contract.

   Should purchaser fail to perform this contract promptly on his part, at the time and in the manner herein specified, the earnest money paid as above shall, at the option of the seller, be forfeited as liquidated damages, and this contract shall be and become null and void. Time is of the essence of this contract, and of all the conditions thereof.

   This contract and the said earnest money shall be held by Lake Title and Trust Company   for the mutual benefit of the parties hereto.

   In testimony whereof, said parties hereto set their hands, this 15th   day of September   , 2001   .

_____ (SEAL)   _____ (SEAL)

_____ (SEAL)   _____ (SEAL)

Loans to purchase real estate are made by savings and loan banks, mutual savings banks, commercial banks, and mortgage banking companies. Buyers that belong to credit unions may find these an additional source of funds. The federal government also has programs that help those who are buying homes. Buyers who have served in the armed forces may qualify for a Veterans Administration (VA) loan, while buyers below certain income levels may be able to receive a Federal Housing Authority (FHA) loan. These loans must be obtained from local lenders, but they are offered at lower rates than conventional mortgages.

Another alternative source of funds is the seller. Under such agreements, the seller acts as the lender in the sale by allowing the buyer to pay for at least a portion of the sales price in installment payments over a specified period instead of paying the entire price at closing.

Since most buyers are not acquainted with lending practices or sources of financing, the real estate professional should be able to advise them on possible loan sources. A successful agent should know the banks and mortgage brokers in his or her area that are making housing loans and those that would be the most favorable to the buyer. This is particularly important during periods of high interest rates and limited availability of mortgage funds.

The real estate agent should also know how to help the buyer determine what amount should be borrowed and whether the buyer will qualify for a loan. It may be difficult for some buyers to obtain a large enough loan. In such cases the real estate agent will be called upon to negotiate the installment contract and point out to the seller the advantages of this type of arrangement.

Closing the Sale

Even if the seller and buyer sign the contract and the buyer locates financing, the transfer of the property is not complete until the sale is closed. In many cases this closing takes place at an actual meeting of the buyer and seller where the money is paid and the deed and other necessary papers are signed. In some states, particularly those in the western United States, the actual transfer is handled by an escrow company. This company acts as a third party for the buyer and the seller. The parties give the necessary papers and monies to the escrow agent, and the agent then checks the materials and distributes the monies and documents to the correct parties.

Whether the closing of the sale is conducted in a face-to-face meeting or through an escrow company, the real estate agent has much of the responsibility for seeing that all the tasks required for the transfer are performed. In some cases the closing is handled by the real estate closer employed by the title company that does the title search or by the financial institution making the loan. But the real estate agent should still do everything possible to ensure that all of the information needed for the closing is completed correctly. For example, some states require inspections for environmental hazards, such as radon and lead-based paint. The agent must ensure that all required inspections and notifications have been completed properly. The agent should be certain that the title company or an attorney checks the seller's title to the property. The lawyer must determine that the seller does in fact own the property and that no other people have any unknown ownership rights to the property. (The work of title officers and lawyers is discussed in Chapter 7.) The agent is also responsible for making certain that the deed is properly registered with the state and that any required transfer or tax stamps are attached to the deed before it is registered.

The real estate broker or salesperson must see that any special terms of the sales contract are carried out before the sale is closed. For example, if the seller has agreed to have the roof fixed, the broker must be sure that this is done. Otherwise the sale cannot be completed. Although many of the activities necessary to complete the sale are handled by attorneys or other persons, the agent must check to be sure that they are actually performed.

Finally, if the sale is going to be closed in a meeting between the parties, the broker or salesperson may be expected to arrange for the meeting and inform all concerned parties. At the closing the deed will be transferred and the sales price paid to the seller. In addition, an accounting, or settlement statement, will be given to both the buyer and seller. The settlement shows the sales price due from the buyer minus any credits, such as unpaid real estate taxes or utility bills. The statement also shows the amount of money that the seller will finally receive once the expenses of the sale have been subtracted. These expenses include the lawyer's fee for preparing the transfer deed, the cost of checking the title, and the real estate agent's commission on the sale. In some cases this settlement statement is prepared by the real estate broker representing the firm. In other cases it is prepared by the seller's attorney, the real estate closer, or the official of the savings and loan making the mortgage loan. In any case, the real estate broker should check the statement for arithmetical errors to be sure that all charges are entered. The closing itself may be conducted by the real estate broker whose firm made the sale. Some state laws limit the abilities of a real estate salesperson to conduct a closing, although he or she should always be present at the meeting.

Additional Responsibilities of Real Estate Brokers

Since many real estate brokers engage in selling activities, they will often perform all of the jobs described in the preceding sections. However, brokers, especially if they own or manage a real estate office, will have additional responsibilities.

The primary responsibility of the broker in a real estate office is supervision of the office salespeople. As we have pointed out, every real estate salesperson must be associated with a supervising broker to work in the real estate field. People who have brokers' licenses but are not owners or supervisors of offices, often called broker-salespeople, also must work under a broker.

Depending on the working of the state's licensing law, the supervising broker has some type of legal responsibility for the actions of the salespeople he or she supervises. If a salesperson commits an illegal action or an error that causes the invalidity of the sale, a broker is often held as responsible as the salesperson. For these reasons, it is important that the broker constantly review the transactions of the salespeople.

The supervising broker's other responsibilities to the office's salespeople are similar to those of any manager in any field. He or she must provide guidance and direction to the salespeople. The broker or the sales manager under his or her direction often conducts training sessions for the salespeople to help improve their skills. The broker must also evaluate the performances of the salespeople and determine if they are producing enough sales and listings to be profitable additions to the office.

The broker's supervisory job is complicated by the independent contractor relationship that usually exists between the salesperson and the firm. The broker cannot set specific work hours for sales-people, require that they participate in training sessions, or request that they work on selling certain properties. In spite of these limitations, the broker must be sure that at least one salesperson is on duty at all times and that all of the listings get sufficient attention. In addition to supervising the salespeople, many brokers are responsible for overseeing the work of the clerical staff and other personnel employed by the firm, including accountants and marketing specialists.

In addition to his or her supervisory responsibilities, most brokers handle many of the administrative duties for the real estate office. He or she must be sure that new listings are posted for the sales staff and sent to the multiple listing service; that "for sale" signs, stationery, and contract forms are available to the salespeople; and that the office area is maintained. If the broker is also the firm's owner, he or she must work with accountants and lawyers on the firm's financial and tax bookkeeping.

Another important function usually handled by the broker in a small office is the creation and placement of advertisements. He or she must decide which of the properties currently listed will be advertised. Often he or she will decide when to schedule open houses for listed property. The broker will also determine how much advertising for the firm, often called institutional advertising, will be done. He or she will have the major responsibility for planning how the firm's image will be presented to the public and what activities will be used to publicize the firm as a whole. If he or she is the owner of the firm, the broker will also decide on what percentage of the firm's income will be spent on advertising. While about 15 percent of the income is considered average for residential offices, the amount and type of advertising will vary depending on the firm's location, competition, and years in the business.

The extent of a broker's supervisory and administrative obligations will depend on the size and income of the office. A common maxim in real estate is that a broker should have either fewer than five salespeople or more than fifteen. This is based on the belief that a broker supervising fewer than five salespeople will have enough time to continue selling and that a broker with more than fifteen salespeople should have enough income to be able to pay a salary to a full-time broker-manager to supplement the income he or she loses by not selling. Larger offices will also be more likely to afford the services of bookkeepers, sales managers, technology specialists, and marketing managers who will perform some of the duties that are handled by a broker in a small office.

Sales Manager

In some larger firms, the supervising broker will not have to perform all of the duties discussed above. Larger firms may employ several experienced agents who will devote some or all of their time to performing one or more of the aforementioned tasks. Many larger firms have a full- or part-time sales manager. The sales manager is responsible for helping to instruct the firm's salespeople in selling and listing techniques that will enable them to do their jobs better. The sales manager may conduct regularly scheduled training sessions, including lectures and role playing in which salespeople practice acting in worklike situations. Often sales managers use material prepared by the National Association of REALTORS; by the franchise, if the firm is a member; or by private real estate publishers.

Marketing Manager

Marketing or advertising managers work on a full- or part-time basis for larger real estate firms. These agents are responsible for planning the advertising and publicity activities of the firm in conjunction with the advertising agency, the supervising brokers, and the firm's owners. The extent of the advertising manager's responsibilities will, of course, depend on the amount and type of advertising the firm does. The manager may simply be responsible for writing the firm's weekly classified ads and seeing that they appear in the local papers. On a more advanced level, the marketing manager may either develop or work with an advertising agency in developing larger ads, brochures, and other material used by the firm. The development of the company's website is also the responsibility of the marketing manager. The amount of this work will depend greatly on the firm's advertising budget and the sophistication of its advertising program. If the firm belongs to a franchise, the advertising manager must also work with the advertising materials provided by the franchise.

In addition to advertising activities, the marketing manager may be responsible for obtaining publicity for the firm. This work may simply involve preparing press releases on new employees for the local paper. The manager may also promote new projects undertaken by the firm or recent achievements of the firm or its salespeople. And the marketing manager may be responsible for promoting any community or civic activities in which the firm engages. For example, if several of the firm's salespeople participate in the local charity drive, the advertising manager should be certain that the salespeople are aware of the information and use it in promoting the firm to prospective clients. The manager will try to interest the local paper in running a story about the salespeople's activities and their connection with the firm.

Financial Manager

Some larger firms employ a full-time financial manager while others rely on outside accountants. The financial manager may be responsible for budgeting the firm's expenses, controlling costs, and keeping records for taxes and financial statements. In recent years there seems to be a much greater emphasis in real estate on using more advanced business and accounting procedures. For this reason the need for competent financial managers will probably increase in the future.

The Broker-Salesperson Relationship

The independent contractor relationship between a broker and a salesperson places certain limitations and responsibilities on each party. Since 90 percent of agents work as independent contractors, these obligations can affect the working life of the real estate agent. Independent contractor status gives the broker less control over the actions of the salesperson than under an employee-employer relationship. The broker has only a limited authority to direct the activities of the salesperson. In order to meet IRS requirements for independent contractors, brokers are not permitted to require the salesperson to conform to any office regulations or procedures such as working certain hours, dressing in a certain manner, or performing certain types of work. The broker may suggest a given course of action to the salesperson, but he or she has no power to direct the salesperson to work in this way. In addition to the limits placed on the broker, the independent contractor relationship places certain responsibilities on the salesperson that are not assumed by employees. The most important of these responsibilities is the salesperson's responsibility to pay the federal government his or her own income tax withholding and social security payments. When a person works as an employee, the money for these payments is subtracted from the paycheck by the company and paid directly to the government. This service is not provided to the independent contractor. Instead he or she must designate a portion of his or her income to cover these costs.

In addition to tax obligations, the salesperson also must set up his or her own health and retirement plans, since these benefits cannot be offered to those working as independent contractors. These types of benefits are often offered by employers at little or no cost to the employee, but the real estate agent must generally pay for them out of his or her income. However, some firms do offer group rate plans to agents. Because of government regulations, independent contractors are often able to qualify for deductions for IRAs (individual retirement accounts) and other types of programs designed for the self-employed.

As an independent contractor, the real estate agent must assume the expenses for materials and tools he or she needs to do business. For example, salespeople must usually provide their own cars for showing property to prospective buyers. Most companies reimburse their employees for transportation expenses, but federal law prohibits independent contractors from receiving such reimbursements. Of course, salespeople can usually deduct a portion of their business expenses from their income tax payments. Federal laws on these deductions are complex, and the agent should consult a tax specialist before taking business deductions.

The Firm's Contribution

In general, real estate firms do provide certain supplies and services to their agents. Most offer secretarial services.

To help salespeople promote their firm during listing or selling presentations, many firms supply brochures or booklets that give background on the firm and highlight the firm's selling points. Some offices may supply entire "listing kits" to salespeople. These kits often include "for sale" signs, brochures on the firm, listing contract forms, information for the prospective seller, and other materials that may be helpful to the salesperson. Most firms provide preprinted listing contracts, sales contracts, and other forms for use by its salespeople. Many firms will also provide items used for open houses such as tables, chairs, and coffee urns. Traditionally, at least some of these services have been provided by the office. The cost of these items is covered by a portion of the salesperson's commission that is paid to the broker. The office's portion of the commission also pays for the other expenses of running the office. These expenses, often called desk costs, are the office's estimate of its expenses divided by the number of salespeople working in the office. The term comes from the idea that every salesperson must sell enough property to pay for the use of his or her desk. Average desk costs can total $16,000 or more annually, depending on the location and size of the business.

Another way that brokers and salespeople divide the cost of doing business is with the 100-percent-commission plan. Under this plan, the salesperson who has sold a certain amount of property receives 100 percent of any commission he or she earns. Unlike more traditional compensation plans, the brokerage receives no commission. Instead, the salesperson pays the brokerage firm a monthly fee to cover the use of the office, secretarial services, and other facilities. For the firm, this system offers the advantage of a steady income regardless of the sales made that month. On the other hand it tends to limit the amount that the firm can earn in any period. For the salesperson, the 100-percent-commission plan can be very profitable if he or she sells enough properties to more than cover the monthly fee. However, in months where the salesperson has few sales, he or she will still have to pay the brokerage fee. Of course, the listing person receives part of the commission.

A new trend in real estate is called "fee for services." Under this type of arrangement, agents and brokers may charge a flat fee for providing certain types of services, for example, negotiating a contract, placing an ad for the property in the newspaper, or conducting an open house for the property. Depending on the agreement, these fees may take the place of the traditional commission when the house is sold. This practice is not widespread, but some sellers like it as an alternative way to save money. Agents benefit from the arrangement because they are guaranteed of receiving compensation for their time, even if the property does not sell.

A broker and the firm he or she represents is a very important part of the salesperson's job. Although some of the relationships are dictated by law, the policies of the office and the personality of the supervising broker are the things that will determine how well a salesperson can do with his or her job. And more importantly, these factors affect how happy he or she is while doing it.

6

REAL ESTATE SPECIALTIES*

SINCE RESIDENTIAL SALES account for approximately 76 percent of all real estate firms, it is very likely that your first job may be in residential sales. However, real estate offers opportunities in a variety of areas. Some brokers and salespeople specialize in selling and leasing commercial properties such as office buildings and stores. Other brokers concentrate on locating, selling, and leasing industrial sites for companies. Another segment of the industry works primarily in locating and selling farms and undeveloped land. In addition to agents who work principally in selling and listing property, there are other real estate specialists who concentrate on managing and leasing property. These managers may be employed as anything from the resident manager of a small apartment to the regional manager of a portfolio of commercial properties. Still other brokers and salespeople are employed in evaluating property

*Statistics in this chapter are taken from the *2001 Membership Profile* and the *1999 NAR Profile of Real Estate Firms* published by the National Association of REALTORS.

for buyers and lenders. The increasingly important role of real estate in the public markets has created opportunities for real estate analysts and investment specialists.

Each of these areas concentrates on a different type of property and requires special knowledge. However, it is not unusual to find brokers and salespeople who work in more than one area. For example, in smaller communities, one brokerage office may sell and lease residential, commercial, and farm properties. Commercial, industrial, and residential brokers often counsel investors as well as locate buyers or tenants for their properties. It is common for sales agents to use some appraisal techniques to evaluate the homes they sell and lease. There is a great deal of overlap, but for the purposes of this book we will talk about each of these real estate areas as a separate specialty.

Residential Brokerage

Since we have already devoted Chapter 5 to a description of the day-to-day activities of the residential sales agent, this section will offer only a brief review.

Residential brokers and salespeople are engaged in the selling and listing of single-family homes, condominiums, and cooperative units. Although some people may buy units, particularly condominiums, as an investment, the majority of the residential broker's business comes from people who are looking for a place to live. Some buyers are very knowledgeable, but many buyers have little or no experience in buying a home, so residential real estate agents should be familiar with all aspects of home buying. The Realtors Residential Sales Council offers the Certified Residential Specialist (CRS) designation and Managers Council offers the Certified Residential Brokerage Manager (CRB) designation to those who have completed specific educational requirements. The Real Estate Buyers Agent Council (REBAC) offers the Accredited Buyers Representative (ABR) to agents who have taken courses in working with buyers.

Residential real estate agents devote their workdays to soliciting listings and showing listed properties to prospective buyers.

Some agents work on a part-time basis, although this is much less common than it was a few years ago. Quite a few agents who work in commercial or industrial brokerage or development as well as in other specialties began their careers in residential sales. Other agents may work in residential sales for their entire working lives and find both financial rewards and job satisfaction. Most residential real estate salespeople work as independent contractors and are paid a commission on the sales they make instead of a regular salary. With the average sales price of a single-family home at $139,000 in late 2000, a commission of 5 to 7 percent on a sale will give the brokerage firm a commission of about $6,950 to $9,730. Of course, portions of the commission are given to the agent who listed the property and to the brokerage firm for which the selling agent works. However, on a commission of around $8,000, the real estate agent is likely to receive a commission of between $2,000 and $3,000. If a salesperson can sell about $1 million worth of property in a year, he or she should have an annual salary of between $35,000 and $60,000.

Commercial Brokerage

Commercial property is usually defined as income-producing property. The term covers many of the properties used by business either as offices or as retail or service facilities. The term may include every type of structure—restaurants, shopping malls, office buildings, warehouses, and parking lots. Commercial property also includes apartment buildings and residential units that are leased to residents other than the owner to produce income for the owner.

About 6 percent of real estate brokers active in the field are engaged in the sales and leasing of commercial property as their principal activity. Like residential brokers, commercial brokers and salespeople devote a great deal of their time to selling and listing property. They advertise property and show it to prospective buyers, either as representatives of the buyer or the seller. However, unlike residential brokers, most commercial clients are investors buying the building as a source of income rather than for their own use. For this reason, commercial buyers are interested in return on investment and expenses as well as the condition of the building and its location.

In order to assist buyers in evaluating the investment potential of a property, commercial agents will often conduct feasibility studies on the property. A study will show probable expenses in maintaining the property, taxes, and other costs. It will also estimate possible income that can be realized on the property. The report shows the buyer what the possible uses of the building are and what types of firms or individuals might be interested in leasing the building. In order to complete a feasibility analysis, a commercial broker gathers information on the current zoning of an area and on the projected growth of the neighborhood. He or she will also take into account the taxes on the property and the income tax charges that affect the return that the investor can achieve. The complexity of the feasibility statement depends on the size of the property and the demands of the potential investors. Obviously the study for a six-unit apartment building will not be as detailed as one for a regional shopping mall. In some cases, the feasibility study will be done by the agent. In other cases real estate appraisers and investment specialists may be employed by the commercial broker to compile the information. In either case, the commercial agent must be knowledgeable about the information in the analysis so that he or she can discuss and explain the reports with the client. Brokers must be aware of available financing as well as which financing method will be the most beneficial to the buyers and sellers for each transaction.

Because of the range of properties handled by commercial brokers, potential clients encompass both individual investors and large institutions and syndicates. Institutional investors include insurance companies, pension funds, and companies that want to diversify their holdings into real estate. Individuals may either buy smaller properties as sole owners or buy a portion of larger properties as members of a partnership. In a partnership, most investors do not take an active part in the management of the property. In some cases commercial brokers may be hired by investors to locate potential investment properties, or by tenants of commercial buildings to locate appropriate space for their businesses. Commercial brokers may also be expected to provide property management services for investment buildings that they have sold. For this reason, many commercial brokerage firms either have a property management division or work in association with a property management firm that will provide these services. (Property management responsibilities will be discussed later in this chapter.)

Background and Working Conditions

Since commercial real estate agents work more closely with feasibility studies and income estimates than do residential agents, they generally need to have more substantial backgrounds in business, accounting, and finance than do residential agents. Commercial agents need to have good mathematical aptitude and a skill for detailed work to collect and organize the larger amounts of factual information that are used in doing feasibility studies. They must also have systematic, logical minds that are able to grasp all of the elements of the study and draw correct conclusions from the material.

Another factor that contributes to the success of commercial real estate brokers is their familiarity with business practices and procedures. Since many commercial clients are business managers, corporate finance officers, or other executives, commercial agents must be able to anticipate the types of questions and problems that will arise in dealing with these individuals. And since many listing and sales presentations are made in corporate settings, it is essential that the commercial broker feels comfortable in dealing with those in management positions. As with all areas of real estate, good communication skills and the ability to work easily with people are necessary for commercial agents.

Many commercial agents come to the field from work in finance, marketing, business sales, or residential real estate sales. Because of the emphasis on economics and finance in the sale of commercial real estate, agents should have some courses in business, finance, marketing, and business law. Valuable training in commercial transactions is also available through the Certified Commercial Investment Member Institute, an affiliate of the NAR with approximately twelve thousand members and candidates for membership. This organization offers courses and publications geared to marketing commercial properties, completing feasibility analyses, and developing management techniques. The organization offers designations such as the Certified Commercial Investment Member (CCIM) to members who have met certain education and experience requirements.

In general, commercial real estate agents work on a straight commission basis. But since some commercial transactions may take a long time to complete, often several months to several years, some new agents may be paid a salary until they gain experience in the field. Commissions on commercial sales range from 2 to 10 percent of the sale price depending on the complexity of the transaction and the size of the property. Professionals engaged in commercial leasing on behalf of either owners or tenants usually receive a commission of between 5 to 7 percent of the rent. Commercial brokerage firms usually charge a flat fee for consultation work to advise investors on possible investment properties and occasionally for selling large properties. Commercial brokers will usually receive a portion of the fee based on the amount of work they do on the transaction. According to a recent NAR survey, commercial brokers had average earnings of about $60,000.

Opportunities for Women and Minorities

According to the *Occupational Outlook Handbook*, 1998–99, more than half of the 347,000 real estate agents and brokers in the United States were women. In commercial and industrial sales this proportion is quite different. Job opportunities for both women and ethnic minority groups have increased over the past decade, but white males hold the large majority in all companies and jobs.

Nevertheless, only a decade ago, it was rare for either women or individuals in minority groups to be represented at all in this field. Today members of both groups are seen in sales, management, and ownership of commercial and industrial real estate firms, and the numbers have been growing.

Because commercial and industrial sales and leasing involve knowledge of fire and safety regulations, shipping and transportation needs, local traffic patterns, commercial and industrial zoning, and a broad range of specialized skills, newcomers to the field come often as the result of related work experience. As more women and minority groups become part of industrial and commercial management and ownership, more of them will find positions in industrial and commercial real estate as well.

Industrial Brokerage

Industrial brokerage activity is concerned with the buying, locating, and selling of manufacturing facilities, warehouse and distribution space, research and development facilities, and other properties used by industry. Agents help to locate and/or develop industrial sites that are suited to the demands of a particular type of industry. In recent years many commercial and industrial developers have specialized in constructing custom "built-to-suit" properties for corporations. They also may work with owners and developers to lease or sell existing properties to industries that need special facilities. Because many industries may have very specialized demands, it is essential that industrial brokers and salespeople be knowledgeable about the demands of the industries they serve. For example, many manufacturing industries need to be near to the source of their raw materials and to highways and railroads so that the raw materials can be easily transported to the facility and the finished goods away to market. Distribution facilities must be centrally located near highway, rail, and air connections. Other firms may have special requirements for their machinery such as large amounts of floor space and large amounts of power or water. Printing plants have to have enough space for their large presses and floors that are strong enough to support the heavy machinery. This is the reason that newer printing facilities are often built in outlying areas where large amounts of available land make it possible to build facilities with all of the floor space on one level. Industrial brokers must also be aware of building and zoning regulations that may limit building.

Industries are also interested in locating in areas with a large labor pool. As part of their need for labor, industrial clients expect industrial realtors to be knowledgeable about recreational, cultural, and housing facilities in the areas they are considering. Industries believe that they are more likely to attract enough employees if they locate in areas that offer amenities that are attractive to those workers. This is especially true of businesses that do not need large special facilities. For this reason, industrial brokers, like other real estate brokers, must be familiar with the communities in which they operate.

In addition to a knowledge of diverse industries and their needs, industrial real estate agents must have expertise in financing and in the suitability of different types of financing to the needs of the company. Among the most common types of financing used by industrial purchasers is the "sale-leaseback." Under this method, the industry using a facility constructs the building to meet its specifications. The firm then sells the property to one or more investors and leases the property back from the investors on a long-term lease. The technique permits industries with special real estate needs to have the type of property they need without having to have large amounts of money invested in real estate.

As well as selling property, many industrial brokers act as leasing agents for investors and developers of industrial parks and buildings. In some cases, they are also responsible for managing the property after the leasing is completed.

Background and Earnings

Industrial brokers and salespeople may work for firms that specialize in industrial or commercial and industrial brokerage. Some of these firms also work in industrial development while others concentrate on selling and listing. Many larger residential firms are now operating a commercial and industrial division. In addition, some residential firms may engage in some commercial or industrial transactions, especially in rural areas where an industrial real estate firm may not be available. Larger industrial concerns may employ specialists in industrial real estate to locate and manage their property.

Brokers and agents may enter industrial real estate sales through residential or commercial brokerage. Because of the need to be familiar with the requirements of industry, many other industrial agents begin their careers in real estate after working for a particular industry. As with commercial real estate, the need to be familiar with industry real estate needs makes it difficult for agents to enter the field directly from college. After entering the field, industrial brokers and salespeople can obtain additional education from the courses offered by the Society of Office and Industrial Realtors. The society also produces publications that help industrial brokers expand their knowledge of the field.

Like most real estate agents, industrial brokers and salespeople usually work as independent contractors and earn commissions on sales instead of a salary. Commissions may vary depending on the size of the property and how specialized the facilities are. Consultations and locating services are usually handled for a flat fee with the agents involved receiving a portion of the total fee. Because industrial transactions take so long to finalize, it may be three to five years before an industrial broker begins to earn a good income.

At present there are approximately seventeen hundred members of the Society of Office and Industrial Realtors. The limited number of firms engaged in the field restricts the employment opportunities for those interested in entering it. Also, larger corporations may employ industrial brokers to help locate sites for the company's own use. Opportunities for women and minorities in the industrial area tend to be very limited. Of course, there is some possibility of gaining experience in the specialty by working for firms that engage in an occasional industrial transaction.

Farm and Land Brokerage

Although farmland still accounts for a significant percentage of U.S. land, only about 4 percent of all real estate firms specialized in the sale of farms and land in 1999. Brokers and salespeople who are engaged in the farm and land field sell and buy farms for individuals and investors. Agents often work with developers in acquiring land near the edges of cities for use as residential and industrial developments. In order to sell farmland effectively, a farm and land agent should be knowledgeable about soil conditions, drainage, water supplies, climate, and other factors that will affect farm yield. Agents should be acquainted with new advances in technology that change farming procedures. Agents should also be informed about the availability of labor in the area. Clients will need to know about available transportation for shipping produce to markets. In addition, for those farm buyers who will be farming the property themselves, farm and land brokers need to have information on the community and its facilities much as they would for a residential buyer.

However, today, almost all of the farms that are bought in this country are purchased by investors rather than individual farmers. To meet the needs of these investors, farm and land brokers will need to be particularly familiar with the production costs of farming the property, the cost of fuel, and other factors that will have a substantial impact on the profitability of the venture. Brokers should also be able to project the future uses of the land both as farm property and as developments. This is particularly important if the farms being sold are located fairly close to cities. As the cities expand, farmland may become valuable to investors. Since much farm property is bought by investors, many farm brokers also provide management services for farms that they have bought or sold.

Farm and land brokers may also work as appraisers of rural properties. Appraisals of rural property differ substantially from those of urban sites. In addition to evaluating buildings and other improvements, the rural appraiser must evaluate the soil, the water availability, and other conditions that will affect crop yield.

Background and Training

Many brokers and agents who specialize in agricultural land come from farm backgrounds and are familiar with the special requirements of agricultural production. Others may have taken courses in agriculture or farm management. Additional training for those interested in careers in farm and land brokerage is available in courses sponsored by the Realtors Land Institute, an affiliate of the National Association of REALTORS. Community colleges in rural areas may also offer courses in farming and agricultural management. Land brokers who act as farm managers must have experience in controlling costs and managing farm personnel. Land brokers who work primarily in consolidating land for future development must be acquainted with zoning regulations that may affect the development. All land brokers should be familiar with financing available to the developer or the investor. Because many brokers who sell land also sell other types of residential and commercial property, those interested in entering farm brokerage can gain experience in the field by starting to work with a firm that handles a few farm sales.

Like almost all real estate professionals, those selling farms and other land work as independent contractors and receive a percentage of the sales price of properties they market. Those working as farm managers and rural appraisers usually work for a flat fee or, in the case of farm managers, for a percentage of the profits plus a small salary. Although women still make up less than one-half of the eight thousand members of the Land Institute, there are expanding opportunities for women in the field of land brokerage.

Appraisal

One of the most interesting and important real estate specialties is real estate appraisal, the skill of placing a value on a property or piece of land. To some extent all competent real estate salespeople and brokers use appraisal skills when they help sellers analyze their market and place a selling price on their home, land, or commercial property. In a competitive market analysis, the residential real estate broker investigates the property and compares its features to those of other properties that have recently sold in the same area. Based on the sales price of the comparable properties, the agent estimates the probable range of the sales price that the house will currently bring. The agent must be able to accumulate information on the properties and analyze the data to draw conclusions.

However, in many cases, especially when property is bought, taxed, or insured, a more thorough analysis of value is required. In these instances, the bank, the insurance company, the government, the buyer, or the seller will use the services of a real estate appraiser. Appraisers evaluate property for a variety of institutions for a variety of reasons. Federal, state, and local governments must have accurate value estimates of property to assess real estate taxes or inheritance taxes if the property's owner has died. Banks and savings and loans want to be certain that the property on which they are making a loan is worth the amount of that loan. Insurance companies want to be sure that the property they insure is worth the value of the insurance coverage. The government will also need to know the value of property that is being taken over by the state for public improvements such as highways and public buildings. The courts may also require that property be appraised in cases of divorce and bankruptcy. Securities brokers who package groups of properties or mortgages for sale must know the value of properties sold to investors.

Appraisal Techniques

The types of techniques that appraisers use to evaluate property depend on the purpose of the appraisals they are performing. In evaluating residential property for taxation or mortgages, the appraiser most often uses the market data approach. The market data approach analyzes the value of the property using the same techniques as the market comparison analysis discussed in Chapter 5. The appraiser determines the value of a particular property by comparing it with the value of comparable property (see the Comparable Sales Comparison Chart). In comparing the property, the appraiser considers such variables as lot size, lot location, number of rooms, the age and condition of the property, condition of the heating and cooling systems, the property's landscaping, the condition of the neighborhood, and any changes in the area or in the market since the other houses used for comparison were sold. Once he or she has carefully inspected the property to verify the data, the appraiser compares the property to others that have been sold in the same area within a short period. The agent will then add or subtract value depending on how the property in question compares with the other properties analyzed. The appraiser then decides on a specific price for the property.

Another method used by appraisers to evaluate property is the cost approach. The cost approach is based on the cost of replacing the building with an identical structure. The cost approach is most often used in evaluating new buildings or very specialized buildings that would be difficult to compare with other properties in an area.

Still another technique used by appraisers is the income approach. Under this method, the appraiser estimates the future income of the property based on past performance and projected market conditions. He or she then estimates future operating expenses and depreciation, i.e., the future deterioration of the property. The appraiser then subtracts the future costs from the future income to determine what the probable profit on the property will be. This approach is particularly valuable to potential investors and lenders who are concerned with return on the money that is spent for the property.

Work Environment

Some appraisers work for real estate firms or other businesses such as banks, insurance companies, the government, or other organizations that are involved in buying or selling property. These appraisers are employees of the firm and are generally called *staff appraisers*. The 1999 *Occupational Outlook Handbook* estimates that twenty-two thousand people worked as appraisers in 1998. A *Membership Profile*, published by The Appraisal Institute, found that 27.7 percent of its members worked for others. Other appraisers work as independent businesspeople and perform appraisals for firms and individuals on a contract basis. These appraisers usually work as individuals or as part of a small appraisal firm. Appraisers who work directly for the client are usually called *fee appraisers* because they work for a fee. The *Membership Profile* found that 60.2 percent of its members were self-employed and that 82 percent worked as fee appraisers.

Unlike some other kinds of real estate agents, appraisers do not receive a commission on their work. Instead they receive a set fee for each appraisal depending on the complexity of the work. Appraisers who work for institutions usually work more regular schedules than most people in the real estate industry, but independent fee appraisers, like other real estate professionals, usually set their own hours and may work long hours to meet client demands. Since appraisers must inspect property sites as part of the evaluation process, appraisal work may involve some travel and outdoor work.

Because of the different areas of employment in the industry, salaries for an appraiser vary considerably. A beginning appraiser who starts as an apprentice with an established appraiser may earn only about $20,000 a year. A 2000 study by Washington University in St. Louis found that experienced appraisers earned an average of between \$40,000 and \$52,000 a year, depending on their educational level. According to The Appraisal Institute, appraisers who held their Senior Residential Appraiser designation averaged earnings of \$94,049 in 1999. Those without averaged \$68,614.

In its *1999 NAR Profile of Real Estate Firms*, the NAR found that only about 4 percent of its member firms are primarily appraisers. However, the future employment prospects for appraisers are stronger than for many other real estate specialties since employment is not so closely tied to the conditions of the market. Women and minorities still account for only a small percentage of appraisers.

Education and Qualifications

Beyond holding a real estate license there are no legal requirements to act as an appraiser in most states. However, to gain success in the field, the appraiser must have extensive knowledge of a variety of areas. Many colleges and private real estate schools offer one or more courses in appraisal either as part of a degree program or as preparation for a broker's license. Excellent courses in a variety of appraisal techniques are offered by the Appraisal Institute. This organization also offers designations such as the Member, Appraisal Institute (MAI) and the Specialist, Residential Appraisal (SRA), which can be achieved only through a combination of education and experience. The 2000 study by Washington University cited above found that 64.7 percent of Appraisal Institute members held at least a B.A. degree.

The prospective appraiser will also need many of the same communications and client-contact skills as other real estate agents. In

Comparable Sales Comparison Chart

	Subject Property	Comparables				
		1	2	3	4	5
Sale Price		$79,000	$93,500	$84,500	$85,000	$93,000
Location	quiet street	+$900				
Age	8 years					
Size of Lot	75' × 200'					
Landscaping	good					
Construction	brick			+$600		
Style	colonial					
No. of Rooms	8					
No. of Bedrooms	3				−$5,000	
No. of Baths	2	+$3,000	+$3,000	+$3,000	+$3,000	
Sq. Ft. of Living Space	1600					
Other Space (Basement)	full bsmt.					
Condition—Exterior	good					
Condition—Interior	good					
Garage	2-car attd.					
Other Improvements						
Financing						
Date of Sale			+$7,100			
Net Adjustments	+$12,000					
Adjusted Value	$91,000					

addition, appraisers must be knowledgeable about taxation, financing, computer operations, and management. Perhaps most importantly, appraisers must be talented in gathering and analyzing information. Appraisers should combine good research skills with sound judgment in evaluating and reporting on property. Familiarity with economics, accounting, and mathematics also will be beneficial to the prospective appraiser.

Appraisal offers a rewarding and diversified career for those who are interested in the analytical aspects of the real estate industry. Although this book focuses on the appraisal of land and real property, appraisers also work in other areas where goods must be valued including art, gems, and equipment.

Property Management and Leasing

Another area of specialization that exists alongside real estate sales is the field of property management. We have already mentioned under commercial, industrial, and land brokerage, that those people who sell property also may be engaged in the management of that property. While this is often the case, especially for smaller properties or for those located in outlying areas, more and more real estate professionals are beginning to specialize in the management of property rather than in sales.

Property managers are responsible for overseeing the leasing and operation of buildings ranging from apartments and condominiums to shopping centers and office buildings. Other agents may specialize in managing farms, industrial buildings, or public housing projects. Property managers, or facilities managers, may also manage property owned and used by their corporate employers. While managers may work with several types of property, especially in smaller areas, many agents in urban areas specialize in one or two types.

Managers' Duties

Depending on the type of property and the degree of the manager's expertise, he or she may have a variety of responsibilities. Managers of residential property may begin their careers as resident managers who live on the premises and handle the day-to-day operations of a large apartment or condominium complex. Resident managers are often responsible for advertising and renting the apartments, collecting rents, handling routine tenant demands, supervising the maintenance staff, handling security, and maintaining routine budget and expense reports. Resident managers must have good organizational skills and the ability to work with people on a regular basis. Facilities managers may also supervise space planning, furniture purchasing, and other areas relating to employee space use.

As the property manager gains more experience, he or she will acquire more and more responsibility in managing all aspects of a property. Experienced property managers may supervise several resident managers, hire all personnel that works on the buildings such as cleaning and maintenance staffs, and buy all supplies used by the buildings. Experienced managers are usually responsible for handling all financial payments for the building including taxes and mortgage payments. They also may advise the property's owners on necessary improvements to maintain the value of the building. Managers must be familiar with laws and regulations governing tenant rights, housing codes, and lease agreement provisions. The manager must be knowledgeable about controlling costs and maximizing profits for the owners while maintaining the value of the property.

Commercial property managers who work on office buildings, shopping centers, and other income-producing properties perform many of the same duties as residential managers. Commercial managers must be adept at making alterations to existing commercial space to meet the needs of the new tenants without incurring considerable costs. Commercial property managers also must be able to write effective leases that will satisfy tenant needs. Lease provisions vary considerably for commercial properties. In many cases, lease payments are negotiated to include both a fixed rent and a percentage of the profits realized by the store; this is particularly common in large shopping center rentals. Tenants of industrial properties also are often responsible for maintaining the property that they lease. In some cases, the industrial property manager may work directly for the company leasing the site. Or, the industrial manager may work for the owners of the industrial park and be responsible for overseeing the properties of several industries. Facilities managers for corporations may be responsible for site selection, interior space planning, property sales, and other issues relating to a corporation's property needs.

Work Environment

Property managers must spend large amounts of time on the premises of the property or properties that they manage. They must be present to show apartments or offices, handle tenant problems, and oversee personnel. In addition, higher level property managers must devote considerable office time to financial planning and administration. Regional property managers for large national firms may oversee the operations of many properties and report on their overall financial performance to investors. The 1999 *Occupational Outlook Handbook* estimated that there were 315,000 people engaged in property management. A 1997 survey by the Institute of Real Estate Management (IREM) found that 40.7 percent of its members worked for a property management company and 35.4 percent worked for a full-service real estate company. Over 39 percent of those surveyed worked for a firm with ten or fewer employees, although the "typical" management company had eleven to twenty employees.

According to the 1999 NAR survey, about 6 percent of the organization's members are engaged in the management of property. This number may in fact be higher as many sales offices also handle some property management as a secondary enterprise. While most property managers work as independent contractors for real estate firms, some work either for the industry or the apartment building association that they manage. Some property managers are paid a flat fee for their services. Others work for a percentage of the gross or net revenues received from the property. This percentage can range anywhere from 3.5 to 6 percent depending on the type of the property. The 1997 IREM survey found that its members received an average total compensation of $86,362. The 1999 *Occupational Outlook Handbook* found the average for all property managers was $29,930.

Educational Requirements

Most states require that property managers hold real estate licenses to work in the field. Some states exempt resident managers of small apartment buildings from the licensing requirements. Persons who manage larger public housing projects under the guidance of the federal government must also hold a certificate from the Department of Housing and Urban Development. Courses in property management are often offered by colleges and private schools either as part of a degree program in real estate or as preparation for a broker's licensing examination. Courses in many aspects of property management are also offered by trade associations such as the Institute of Real Estate Management (IREM), an affiliate of the NAR; the Building Owners and Managers Association; and also the International Council of Shopping Centers. The institute offers the Certified Property Manager (CPM) designation and the Accredited Residential Manager (ARM) award to members who have met specific educational and experience requirements. Respondents to the 1997 IREM survey found that 51.2 percent of its members held college degrees and another 18.9 percent had completed a graduate degree. Slightly over 76 percent of respondents had fourteen or more years in the property management business. The median number of years in the business was 18.4.

Opportunities for Women

Property management is a field that offers considerable opportunity for women. The 1997 IREM survey found that 33.8 percent of its members and 49.1 percent of its candidates for membership were women. Many women work as residential property managers. Experience in management can be gained by working for sales firms in the residential or commercial field that manage a few properties as a supplemental service. The field also offers both entry possibilities as resident managers for those just beginning in real estate and a source of supplemental income for retired individuals. Although the opportunities in commercial management are not as extensive, job openings in this area are increasing.

Development

The real estate developer is really the jack-of-all-trades of the real estate industry. He or she is responsible for every step of the process involved in turning raw land into housing developments, shopping centers, and industrial parks. To do this the developer should have at least some knowledge of every area in real estate from site selection and construction through financing to marketing. Of course, many developers hire builders, salespeople, and real estate consultants in special areas to help them in making their decisions. But the land developer is responsible for holding the whole project together. In recent years, development demand has slowed for many property types, with the exception of single-family homes. As a result, many developers have begun managing the properties they develop.

Probably the most difficult and important task performed by the real estate developer is determining what types of property will be in demand and profitable in any given area. The developer must analyze future markets to project income and population for the area. He or she must also know about the future construction of highways that will increase or decrease the accessibility of the project. The developer must consider the possible construction of other types of developments in the same area and whether these will benefit his or her enterprise or compete with it. For example, if a developer plans to build a shopping center in an outlying area of a city, the news that other developers are building residential developments in the area will be an asset. But if this same developer is planning a subdivision, he or she must reconsider the planning to decide if the area's growth will be large enough to absorb that many additional housing units.

Site Selection and Building

After determining the feasibility of the planned development, the developer must select a site for the project and supervise the construction of the buildings and other improvements. In selecting a site, the developer must consider the existing zoning laws of an area; the available roads leading to the site; the availability of sewer, water, and power lines that will be needed; and the environmental regulations governing the area. Especially if the development is large, the developer may work out an agreement with the city or county to share the cost of the roads and utilities that will be needed for the area. In some cities, new developments are taxed at a lower rate for a certain number of years to give developers an added incentive for locating in these areas.

Although the developer may supervise the construction and design of the project, he or she hires trained architects and builders to perform these functions. However, because the developer is the person finally responsible for the project, he or she must make the final decision on construction. He or she must also maintain careful control of costs during the construction phase to ensure that a profit will be made on the property.

Financing

Before beginning construction on the project, the developer must undertake the difficult job of finding financing for it. Because of the large amounts of money involved in most development projects, the developer does not use the same types of financing as the average home buyer. Development loans are often funded from insurance companies, pension funds, and other large companies that want to invest a portion of their funds in real estate. In recent years, many development companies have turned to Wall Street and the public markets for funding by selling stock. Many well-known developers have created real estate investment trusts

(REITs) or public real estate operating companies (REOCs) that acquire new capital by selling stock to investors. Development loans usually cover the costs of the construction of buildings and any necessary improvements such as roads and sewers. The total of the loan is often paid out in partial amounts over the course of the construction to provide further protection to the lender. In many cases, repayment of these loans is also made on a partial basis as the lots begin to sell or the stores begin to be rented.

Some developments are financed by partnerships of buyers who pool their money to provide sufficient funds to construct the project.

Marketing

Once the property is completed—or, more often, as soon as construction has begun—the developer must begin the important task of marketing the property. The scope of the marketing effort depends to a large extent on the size and type of the property. For larger properties, developers often produce attractive, expensive booklets, brochures, and other materials that highlight the assets of the property. These may include illustrations of the as yet unfinished development showing how it will look on completion. For commercial properties, developers will include careful analyses of projected customers and anticipated expenses for the facilities. In many states, the developer must file information on the property with a state agency. The agency then verifies the developer's submission to be sure that the consumer's rights are protected and that the property is not misrepresented.

Usually as the project nears completion, the developer will hire one or more salespeople to assist in selling or leasing the property. The number of salespeople will, of course, depend on the size and type of property being offered. Working as a salesperson for a developer can give real estate agents interested in development the opportunity to gain some exposure in the area.

Background and Experience

Developers come to real estate from almost every area. Some have worked in residential or commercial real estate as salespeople or property managers. Others come to development from allied fields such as building or finance, where they have acquired some of the expertise they need to manage the entire development process. In some cases these people may have worked for developers in completing some phase of a project.

Often developers begin with a small project that they finance on their own or with only a few backers. For example, a new developer may buy one or two older homes in an improving city neighborhood and renovate the properties. As the developer gains expertise, he or she will expand operations to include the development of larger and more complex properties. Other developers begin as investors who become interested in the potential of the field and gradually move into the development area. Still others may begin as salespeople or as assistants to established developers and learn the business in this way.

Developers need a good knowledge of financing and marketing techniques in order to attract investors to the project and manage the complex financial arrangements necessary for large undertakings. Marketing expertise is also important in deciding how to publicize and sell the new properties once they are completed. Management skills are essential for REITs and other developers who retain their properties after construction is completed. Persons considering a career in development should take courses in construction, marketing, economics, and land planning to prepare for the many-faceted areas of real estate development. It is also advisable to have at least a few years experience in either real estate or a closely related field before undertaking a development project. Of course, a developer can hire experts in one or more areas, but it is advisable that the developer have some knowledge of all real estate areas. In most states, developers do not have to be licensed, unless they actually sell the property. But most developments must meet with state guidelines, especially if the property is sold to out-of-state buyers.

Earnings

Only about 1 percent of the 1999 NAR membership were classified as developers. However, these real estate professionals have among the highest average earnings of any group in the NAR. In some cases, developers include a salary for themselves as part of the expenses of the project while it is under construction. However, substantial profits cannot be realized until the property is completed and is operating or sold, which may be several years from the time it is first planned. Although the rewards of development are great, the business does involve a great deal of risk. Even with the most extensive market analysis, it is not always possible to predict the state of the economy or the area in the future. This risk is further increased by the large sums of money involved in development and the long period that elapses between the time the project is first planned and the first property is sold or leased.

Corporate Real Estate/Facilities Management

A real estate specialization that has gained more prominence in recent years is that of facilities managers or corporate real estate executives. The 1999 *Occupational Outlook Handbook* estimates that

348,000 people were employed as facilities managers in 1998. These professionals are responsible for buying, selling, building, and managing the real estate owned by corporations. This real estate can include offices, factories, warehouses, research labs, and retail outlets. Because the cost of real estate operations is often a company's second-biggest expense, after personnel, the corporate real estate executive has become an important part of any company.

This professional works with top management and with business units to optimize the best use of real estate so that the company can conduct its business. Corporate real estate executives may look for new sites for factories or warehouses to be built, may review building operations to find ways to save money on heating and other costs, and may negotiate with building owners to obtain space a company needs.

Because of corporate downsizing, facilities managers often work with outside vendors to perform some or all of these functions. They will often hire development or construction companies to build new sites. They will work with cleaning companies, equipment repair firms, interior designers, and a host of other suppliers to ensure that space operates efficiently and at the lowest possible cost. They will work with real estate brokers and leasing agents to buy, sell, or rent space.

Unlike many real estate professionals, corporate real estate executives usually earn a salary from their corporate employer. However, as corporations work to save money, many executives receive bonuses based on lowering expenses.

Education and Background

Many individuals come to corporate real estate management from private development or property management companies. Because the corporate real estate executive oversees a variety of tasks, a diverse background is beneficial.

The corporate executive must deal with other business specialists within a company, so an M.B.A. or other business degree is very useful for this type of position. Experience working in a business other than real estate might also help the corporate real estate executive understand the concerns of corporate finance and planning departments.

Corporate executives must work with a variety of outside suppliers as well as representatives of many corporate departments, so good interpersonal skills are essential. Because part of a facilities manager's role is to help meet the space needs of the company, he or she should be skilled in forming alliances and negotiating agreements between groups.

Salary and Compensation

According to the 1999 *Occupational Outlook Handbook*, administrative services and facilities managers had median annual earnings of $44,370. The top 10 percent earned more than $89,850. Industries paying the highest median salaries were hospitals and commercial banks. According to the International Facility Management Association, facilities managers had earnings of $66,000 in 1998, with top executives earning in excess of $160,000.

A 2000–2001 survey by NACORE International showed that the approximately four thousand members who belong to this corporate real estate group received an average annual compensation of $152,622. Facilities/property managers for corporate real estate departments received an average compensation of $91,673, while construction managers averaged $113,631, according to the survey.

Real Estate Counseling

Real estate counselors are engaged in the business of providing advice on real estate subjects to clients who want assistance in making decisions. In many cases clients use the services of counselors to obtain advice on investments and development of real estate, although counselors can and do provide advice in all areas.

Since counselors are acting as expert advisors they must have a wide-ranging knowledge of all aspects of the real estate industry from land selection to financing. Some counselors specialize in only one type of real estate or engage in counseling in addition to their principal real estate activities. For the most part, counselors have many years of experience in one or more areas of real estate before beginning work as a counselor.

At present few real estate professionals work as real estate counselors on a full-time basis. However, many agents offer some counseling services in addition to their regular sales or management services. Success in real estate counseling depends on the reputation and reliability of the professional. For this reason those who enter the field must have sufficient experience to offer competent guidance to their clients.

Real estate counselors always perform their services for a flat fee. This fee is based on the type and complexity of the work and the experience of the counselor. Many counselors work for clients on a monthly or yearly basis and receive regular payments for their services whether or not the services are used during any particular period. By charging a flat fee rather than accepting a commission on the sale or leasing of property, real estate counselors can guarantee their objectivity in giving advice to clients. Earnings for real estate counselors vary widely depending on the counselor's clientele and whether the counselor is engaged in the activity on a full-time basis.

Additional information on courses and publications on real estate counseling can be obtained from the American Society of Real Estate Counselors. The society also offers a Counselor, Real Estate (CRE) designation to those who have met certain professional standards in the field.

Real Estate Auctioneering

As the name implies, real estate auctioneers sell real estate using auctioneering techniques. Auctioneers may sell any type of property and may sell one lot or a large number of properties. The practice of auctioning property was once used primarily for estate sales and for selling property to satisfy back taxes or an unpaid mortgage loan. However, recently larger numbers of real estate professionals have begun to use auctioneering techniques to sell property. The new phenomenon of online property auctions also has served to increase interest in using auctions to sell property. In general, real estate auctioneers must still hold a real estate license to sell property even if they do not sell property on a full-time basis. Those interested in learning auctioneering skills can obtain additional information on this specialty by contacting the National Auctioneers Association on the Web at auctioneers.org.

7

CAREERS RELATED TO REAL ESTATE

LIKE EVERY PROFESSION in today's society, real estate does not exist in a vacuum. In order to function, real estate professionals must work closely with a variety of other specialists whose jobs interrelate with the real estate field. Real estate sales could not be completed without the loans arranged by mortgage bankers and loan officers. Contracts and title transfers could not be executed without the work of attorneys and title searchers, escrow agents, and real estate closers. The construction of real estate would not be possible without the work of builders, land-use planners, and architects. Real estate investment trusts and mortgages could not be sold without securities brokers.

In some cases, people who work in one of these specialties may also buy or sell real estate in conjunction with their other jobs. Others may begin working in a real estate–related field and gradually shift their working time to real estate. In this chapter we will explore some of the careers closely related to real estate—careers that may provide the first step to a future in real estate.

Loan Officers

Because almost all real estate transactions involve some type of financing, perhaps no field is more closely interconnected with real estate than mortgage lending.

Loan officials may work for banks, independent mortgage banking companies, or mortgage banking divisions of real estate firms. Some loan officials work as mortgage bankers who both negotiate and service the loans. Others work as mortgage brokers who serve as agents between pension funds, insurance companies, and other firms that have money that they want to channel into real estate financing. Still others work to package groups of loans for sale in the financial markets. The 1999 *Occupational Outlook Handbook* estimated that 227,000 people worked as loan consultants in 1998.

Mortgage loan officials are responsible for negotiating loans for a variety of real estate transactions. Loans are made to single family home buyers, to businesses and industries, and to developers who need funds to construct larger projects or make renovations. They obtain and verify information for loan applications and set the terms of the transaction according to their bank's policies. If a conventional real estate mortgage loan will not meet the needs of the borrower, the mortgage officer will suggest alternate types of financing that are available to the borrower and give advice on which type will best meet the individual's needs. He or she will often work closely with the real estate agent involved in the sale to locate sufficient financing to close the transaction. In many cases, loan officials also are responsible for servicing the loan. Servicing the loan includes being sure that all mortgage payments are made, that taxes and insurance payments are made, and that the home is maintained to retain its value. In most cases, loans are not serviced by the same person who negotiated the loan. In fact there are even some companies that contract with banks and savings and loans to service their loans. In some instances, groups of mortgages are "packaged" together and sold to investors. The investors receive income from the long-term mortgage payments while the bank has new money available for loans. These packages of loans are often traded as securities on Wall Street.

Mortgage bankers also may act as agents between developers and insurance companies, pension funds, and other investors who will provide financing for large projects. Banks might make short-term loans to developers to finance properties under construction. Mortgage loan officials might be responsible for negotiating the sale of loans on the secondary mortgage market. In these types of transactions, the bank that originally made the loan sells the right to receive repayment to another investor. This gives the new investor a long-term income and gives the bank funds to make other loans.

Background and Education

Individuals may enter the field of real estate mortgage financing from one of several areas. Some people, especially those who work for the mortgage banking companies or for mortgage banking divisions of real estate firms, have experience in selling or leasing real estate. Other individuals may begin their careers by working in another position in a bank or savings and loan.

In mortgage banking, professionals need experience in financial and economic topics. This experience can be obtained from a baccalaureate or advanced degree in business; from on-the-job training provided by many individual companies; or through such trade organizations as the American Bankers Association and the Mortgage Bankers Association. Since agents negotiate loans between insurance and pension funds and developers, individuals must have strong communications and selling skills similar to those needed in real estate transactions. Although loan officials do not have to hold real estate licenses, at least some experience in the real estate business will be of great assistance to loan officials in evaluating a property before making a loan. Mortgage bankers and brokers will also need to understand the appraisal reports and cash-flow analyses.

Earnings and Working Conditions

Mortgage loan officials work as employees of banks, mortgage banking firms, and mortgage banking divisions of real estate firms. According to the 1999 *Occupational Outlook Handbook*, six out of ten loan officers work for commercial banks. Experts in mortgage finance also may be employed by pension funds, insurance companies, and other firms that place a great deal of their funds in real estate loans. Most loan officials work a conventional workweek of between thirty-seven and forty hours. Evening work and travel may be involved when negotiating loans or meeting with clients from other cities. However, mortgage loan officials have much more regular schedules than most real estate brokers and salespeople.

The majority of real estate loan officials are paid a commission, plus a salary in most cases. Salaries for beginners with no banking experience will vary depending on the applicant's education and the location of the firm.

Salaries for mortgage loan officials may triple or quadruple as individuals gain experience and take on additional responsibilities. In some mortgage brokerage firms, brokers work on a commission basis similar to that used by real estate agents. In these cases the employees receive a commission of anywhere from 25 to 50 percent of the fee charged for making the loan. In 1998, those working full-time as bank loan officers or mortgage bankers earned salaries averaging $34,700 for residential loan officers and $36,400 for commercial loan officers, according to the 1999 *Occupational Outlook Handbook*. Despite the fact that commissioned brokers have greater earning potential than those working for banks on a straight salary basis, they experience many of the same problems with the regularity of income as do real estate professionals.

Opportunities

The demand for loan officers is expected to be higher than average for the next decade. Loans are becoming more complex, and borrowers refinance more frequently. Loan officers also have good job stability as lending is a principle revenue source for most banks.

Title Researchers

In colonial America, titles to property were often transferred without any written record. However, today almost all transfers and transactions affecting real estate are registered with some state agency. Before land is bought, sold, or mortgaged, a professional title examiner almost certainly will "search" the title to be certain that the property is free of prior claims and that there are no doubts about the rights of the present owner to transfer the land. Defects that can make a title difficult to transfer include many minor problems such as a misplaced power line on the property, the failure of one of the signers of an earlier deed to include his or her complete name, or the misspelling of a street name. As you can see, most of these defects are minor and can be corrected by filing an affidavit or other legal statement. But to be certain that the title being transferred cannot later be disputed, the title researcher must note any questionable data.

Title researchers examine and analyze past deeds and other records that are on file with state and county registry offices. Many title insurance companies also maintain their own files for title research. Examiners check lot and map books and look at surveys of the property to be sure that there is no dispute over the boundary lines of the property. They also may check the property in person to be certain that there are no buildings, power lines, or other constructions encroaching on the property. In addition, they will check tax records to be sure all payments have been made.

Examiners usually begin their research by locating the "starter," the most recent acceptable statement of the ownership rights to the title. In some cases, the examiner will not search any records before the starter but will simply concentrate on bringing the title record up to date. In other cases, such as a large transaction or a question on the title, the examiner may search earlier records. Once the examiner has determined any defects in the title, he or she may contact any necessary parties to see if the faults in the title can be corrected. The examiner will maintain contact with the buyers and sellers and their attorneys during these negotiations and consult with them if necessary. Finally the title examiner will write a report analyzing his or her findings. This report will be used by the attorneys and the lenders in deciding if the transaction will be completed. If the buyer in the transaction is purchasing a title insurance policy, the examiner's findings also will be used to determine the terms of the policy. In many cases the same company that conducted the title search will issue the insurance policy.

Title examination procedures vary from company to company. In some cases, title researchers may gather information needed for the search, and title examiners may conduct the actual analysis of the material and write the report on the condition of the title. In other cases the entire procedure may be done by one individual.

Education and Background

There are no specific educational requirements to enter the title field. Some companies hire high school graduates as researchers, although many prefer college graduates with a background in business, accounting, or prelaw. Courses in real estate are also beneficial. Companies hire title researchers directly from school, or they promote clerical employees into title researcher positions. Many title companies provide formal training and courses for new researchers. In most title companies, attorneys are hired to perform some of the more complex title analyses.

Title researchers must combine strong analytical skills and research skills with a good writing ability. Math skills also are necessary to comprehend tax forms and other financial papers. Title searchers must be detail-oriented and able to work independently. Since many title reports must be done rapidly, researchers must be able to work quickly and deal with deadline pressures.

Working Conditions

Title examiners work for a variety of companies that use title information including banks, real estate companies, attorneys, and title insurance firms. Title examiners may also work for federal, state, or local government agencies that condemn property for public use, or they may work for utility companies that purchase land for public improvements. Most title examiners work a conventional forty-hour week, although some overtime may be necessary. Examiners generally work as employees and receive company fringe benefits and paid vacations. In general, title examiners and researchers work in an office environment and spend much of their time working on computers. Some travel may be necessary to check records but most travel will be local.

Earnings for title researchers and examiners vary according to geographical area, size of the company, and experience and education of the individual. Beginning title researchers who conduct research but do not do analyses may earn less than $1,500 a month. Salaries will increase as the researcher gains experience. Top salaries for title researchers will generally be in the low twenties. Beginning title examiners may receive salaries around $25,000. Title examiners with law degrees will generally start at higher salaries than employees with only college training. Senior title examiners may earn upwards of $40,000 to $50,000 a year, especially if their positions include supervision of other examiners.

Job opportunities for both men and women are good for the next few years. The 1999 *Occupational Outlook Handbook* estimated that thirty thousand people worked as title researchers in 1998. Strong real estate sales greatly increase the need for title researchers. Real estate title researching also provides good background for those interested in entering the appraisal field, where the condition of the title may affect the value of the property.

Real Estate Closers and Escrow Officers

Real estate closers and escrow officials are responsible for collecting all of the documents necessary to complete a real estate transaction and for handling all of the funds involved in the transaction. The term *escrow* refers to the process of placing the contracts, deeds, loan money, and other materials involved in the transaction under the care of a person who is not involved in the transaction. The use of a third party to handle the documents and monies involved in a transaction helps to protect the interest of both parties and ensures that the transaction is handled fairly.

In some states, especially those in the west, there are independent escrow companies that perform this function. In some of these states, the buyer and seller of real estate are required to use an escrow company to ensure the honesty of the transaction. In other states, any qualified individual, including the real estate broker involved in the sale, may perform the function of the escrow agent or closer in securing the necessary documents and paying out the money. However, even in states where escrow is not required, these functions are often performed by a real estate closer working for the real estate firm, the title company that is insuring the title, or the financial organization making the loan on the property.

The escrow officer or the real estate closer performs a great many functions connected with the real estate transaction. He or she is responsible for seeing that the title has been searched, any defects found in the title have been corrected, and that title insurance has been issued. The closer also must see that the deed for transferring the property has been prepared, that all necessary inspections and notifications have been carried out, that the loan papers both for taking out the new loan and for paying off the old loan have been completed, that a home owner's insurance policy has been taken out, and that any other arrangements necessary to satisfy the terms of the sale have been completed. Closers and escrow officers also preside over any meetings of the parties when the transaction is closed. They are responsible for being sure that the deed and other documents are properly recorded after the sale is closed.

The escrow agent or closer is also responsible for handling all of the funds involved in the real estate transaction. He or she often holds the money deposited by the buyers when the contract was signed and pays out the money to the seller when the transaction is closed. More importantly, the closer is responsible for calculating the expenses and credits due to each party in the sale. For example, if the buyers have deposited a certain amount of the sales price when the contract was signed, this amount will be credited toward the overall price that they must pay for the house. The closer also calculates what portion of the year's taxes, utility bills, and other costs will be paid by each party. For example, if real estate taxes are paid at the end of the year and the house is sold in July, the sellers will be responsible for the taxes for the half year that they owned the house. However, since they will not own the house at the end of the year, the sellers will pay their portion of the taxes to the buyers when the sale is closed. Then at the end of the year the buyers will pay the amount for the entire year to the taxing agency. The closer is responsible for seeing that the buyers collect this money. After completing the calculations of all expenses and credits, he or she will fill out an accounting statement, called a settlement sheet, that shows the expenses and credits of each party and the final amount due to the sellers. The closer supplies a copy of the settlement sheet to each party.

Education

There are no set educational requirements for becoming a real estate closer or escrow officer, although some state escrow associations, such as that in California, do offer certificates showing that the holder has completed certain educational requirements. Escrow officers and closers may have only a high school degree, although many firms may now prefer to hire those with at least some college education. Because of the work in calculating expenses and credits, the closer should have some background in accounting and strong mathematical skills. Courses in business and real estate law will be helpful, and typing skills are useful for preparing official documents. Since the closer must work with the parties while preparing for the closing and at the closing itself, the closer must have a friendly personality and good communications skills. And, if the need arises, he or she must be able to work with the two parties to resolve any differences that come up.

Real estate closers and escrow officials may begin their careers working for banks as tellers or clerks; as secretaries in escrow offices, title company real estate firms, or law offices; or in similar positions in any company associated with real estate or business. Once an individual is hired as a closer, he or she will receive on-the-job training in the profession. In addition, some state escrow associations offer courses to help those in the field increase their expertise. Consult your state escrow association or land title association for more information.

Working Conditions

Escrow officers and real estate closers may work for independent escrow companies, title companies, savings and loans, or other financial institutions; real estate companies; or builders. They work as employees and receive all benefits offered by the company that employs them. Closers and escrow officers work in a conventional office environment often devoting their working days to telephone contacts and report writing. These employees usually work a regular forty-hour week, although the job often involves some deadline pressures and may require some overtime work.

Depending on their background and experience, beginning real estate closers and escrow officials may receive salaries of between $24,000 to $29,000 a year. Salaries will increase as closers gain more experience in their work and/or move into supervisory responsibilities. Real estate closers also move into more responsible jobs with the companies they work for. For example, closers working for title companies may begin working as title researchers, while those working for lenders may move into positions as loan underwriters.

Urban Planners

Urban, or land-use, planners are concerned with determining how available land can be best used to meet the needs of the community now and in the future. Land-use planners evaluate the community's current housing, schools, hospitals, parks, and other facilities to see if they meet the community's needs. They will also try to project population growth to see if these facilities should be expanded for future years. Planners also examine the businesses and industries in an area to decide if the companies provide enough jobs and goods to meet the demands of the community. They will analyze the location of the industrial and commercial sites to see if their locations fit in with projected growth patterns for the area. Urban and regional planners evaluate transportation, utilities, and other services in an area to see if they will continue to provide necessary services or if they need to be expanded.

Much of the urban or regional planner's work is concerned with projecting how the community will change and estimating its future needs. Planners work with the city or regional governments to decide how these requirements can be met. They may develop drawings and plans of alternate locations for new highways, industrial sites, or housing developments that will both satisfy the community's needs and make the area more attractive and useful for those who live and work there.

The real estate market in any given area is greatly influenced by the work of regional planners. The present or future value and use of property may be affected by the decisions of the planners. For example, if a large industrial development is built near a person's farm, the price of his or her land may increase rapidly, and the owner may make a large profit by selling. Of course, it may make it difficult for the owner who wants to continue to farm his or her land if the property is gradually surrounded by housing developments. Developers must work very closely with regional planners to ensure that new developments coincide with the area's projected growth and use needs. Developers often will consult regional land-use projections before deciding on the location for a proposed development.

Education and Background

Those entering the field of urban or regional planning must have at least a bachelor's degree in city planning, architecture, or engineering. In most cases graduate work in city planning or urban planning is necessary to obtain a satisfactory position. Planners who work for government agencies usually must pass a civil service examination.

Those working in the urban planning field must be able to draw and design physical layouts for developments, use computer programs to analyze land use, analyze urban problems, and develop budgets and other cost estimates for their proposals. Urban planners must be particularly talented in analyzing and evaluating information and in visualizing the eventual outcome of their plans. They must be able to work well with others and to effectively communicate their ideas. In some cases planners also are expected to speak at public hearings or legislative meetings to present their ideas to the public.

Working Conditions and Earnings

Almost all urban and regional planners work for some part of the federal, state, or local government. Or they may work as consultants for large private developers. Planners generally work in a conventional office environment, although they may sometimes have to visit the site to examine the features of the land in question. They usually work a conventional forty-hour week, although some overtime may be necessary. They may also have to travel to meetings, hearings, and other conferences to present their proposals.

Earnings for urban planners vary according to the size of the agency that employs them and their experience and education. According to a 1998 survey by the American Planning Association, planners with fewer than five years of experience had median salaries between $28,000 and $44,000. Planners with more than ten years of experience had median salaries between $37,000 and $86,000, depending on their location.

Surveyors

A profession closely connected with both land-use planning and the development area of real estate is that of the surveyor. Surveyors are responsible for establishing the boundary lines of property and writing legal descriptions of those boundaries. These legal descriptions are used in deeds to establish the exact size and location of the property that is being transferred. The surveyor also notes the size and location of all buildings, water, hills, and other elements of the property. The work of the surveyor is used by the developer in outlining the placement of lots and buildings and by engineers in the construction of roads and other facilities. The surveyor's work is also consulted by title examiners in determining if the property in question is properly described in the deed, and by appraisers in establishing the value of land.

The surveying party, which usually consists of several people, uses electronic and mechanical instruments, such as the theodolite, which is used for measuring angles, to take exact measurements of the property. The surveyor also notes the size and placement of all natural and manmade objects on the property. Surveyors often draw maps showing the location and dimensions of the property and prepare reports of their findings. Surveyors may specialize in areas such as geodetic survey, which measures the subsurface features of the property, to locate water, oil, or natural gas under the property.

Education and Background

Those interested in surveying can enter the field without a college degree, although some degree programs are available. Many colleges and vocational and technical schools offer one-, two-, or three-year courses, or degree programs, in surveying. Experience also can be obtained by working as a surveying assistant on a work team. Those interested in surveying careers should take courses in geometry, algebra, and mechanical drawing. Those who take college work should consider courses in engineering, geology, and the physical sciences. The increased importance of computerized geographic information systems (GIS) in mapping and surveying has made computer skills more important for surveyors. Since surveying often involves outside work in all types of weather, candidates should be in good physical health with no disabilities that would make it difficult for them to work in rough terrain. Accuracy and attention to details are also important, since the surveyor's information is often used for legal purposes.

All fifty states require surveyors to be licensed. However, assistants and those working as part of the surveying team do not have to have a license. Most states require licensed surveyors to have between ten and twelve years experience and to pass an examination to be licensed. In most cases a college degree in a related field may be substituted for a portion of the experience requirements. A few states require surveyors to be college graduates.

Working Conditions and Earnings

Most surveyors work for construction companies, engineering firms, architects, or real estate developers. Others work for federal, state, and local government agencies. Some surveyors may work for independent firms that offer their services to builders and engineers on a fee basis. In some cases surveyors are self-employed.

Surveyors usually work a conventional forty-hour week, although additional work is often done in the summer when weather conditions are better for outside work. A great deal of the surveyor's work is done outside, and he or she may have to travel to reach the site to be surveyed. Because surveyors may have to walk for long distances carrying their instruments, the work can be strenuous and requires physical strength and agility.

Salaries in surveying vary greatly depending on the surveyor's experience. Licensed land surveyors with several years of experience earned salaries averaging $37,640 in 1998. Those working for government agencies averaged salaries of $52,400. A GIS analyst may earn between $26,000 and $48,000, according to the American Congress of Surveying and Mapping. Those with supervisory responsibilities or who own their own firms may earn still more.

Landscape Architects

Landscape architects design the placement of plants, trees, walkways, and other outside elements in parks, office complexes, and residential areas. Landscape architects are concerned with creating attractive environments for the buildings and the people who use them. But they are also interested in designing a landscape that will help to preserve the water and other resources of the area and increase the energy conservation in the buildings. In planning the landscape, these professionals consider the environmental elements of the land including the soil, water, sunlight, and elevation. They also consider the needs of those using the facilities for access to the building and parking for vehicles.

Landscape architects work closely with the architect, engineer, or developer to plan the design of the site. They draw detailed design plans showing the size and location of the vegetation and walkways and boundaries. They also create budgets projecting costs of the construction.

Education and Background

A college degree in landscape architecture is usually required before entering the profession. College programs of four or five years include courses in surveying, drawing, design, mathematics, horticulture, and city planning. English and communication skills are also important because landscape architects must work with clients and architects in developing their plans. And talent and creativity are necessary because much of the landscape architect's work involves design and aesthetic judgment.

In 1999, forty-six states required landscape architects to hold a license before they could work without the supervision of a licensed landscape architect. To take the licensing examination, candidates must generally hold a college degree and have between two and four years of professional experience. The American Society of Landscape Architects can provide additional educational information.

Working Conditions and Earnings

Many landscape architects are self-employed and offer their services to architects and engineers on a fee basis. Others work as employees of builders, developers, architects, landscape building firms, or the federal or state government. In 1998 approximately twenty-two thousand people worked as landscape architects.

Much of the landscape architect's time is spent in a conventional office environment designing and planning. Other portions are spent outside assessing the site and determining the conditions of the environment. Landscape architects who are employees generally work a conventional forty-hour week, but independent consultants may work more hours to meet the demands of their clients. In 1998 experienced architects in the private sector had an average salary of $37,930, according to the 1999 *Occupational Outlook Handbook*. Landscape architects employed by the federal government earned an average of $49,570 annually. Independent landscape architects may earn even greater amounts.

Demand for landscape architects has increased in recent years as more and more people recognize the importance of the outdoor environment. The field offers interesting opportunities for both men and women.

Architects and Builders

Closely related to the real estate field, especially to the areas of development and sales, are the professions of architecture and building. Professionals in these fields are responsible for designing and constructing the homes, office buildings, shopping centers, and factories that are sold and leased by the real estate industry. Architects and builders are often employed by or work in partnership with developers to construct new developments. In some cases the architect may be responsible for hiring the builder and supervising the construction. In other cases the architect and the builder are hired separately by the development company.

Architects are responsible for creating structural and mechanical drawings showing the floor plan of the building and the construction requirements. The architect will also draw in any decorative features he or she believes will enhance the appearance of the building. If the initial design is accepted by the client, the architect and his or her staff will prepare more detailed drawings that show the exact dimensions and composition of the building's elements as well as the placement of plumbing, heating, air conditioning, and other utilities. Architects will also determine the materials that will be used for the interior and exterior areas of the building. In some cases the architect will select the contractor and negotiate the terms of construction. In all cases the architect will make periodic visits to the construction site to be sure that the work is being carried out according to the plans. In 1998 approximately ninety-nine thousand people were licensed as architects.

Builders who work as general contractors are responsible for supervising all areas of the building's construction. They will hire the carpenters, plumbers, electricians, and other construction workers who are needed to complete the building according to the architect's plans. In many cases general contractors hire subcontractors who perform one or more of the jobs needed in the building. Builders must supervise the buying of the materials and be certain that they are shipped and stored to be used as needed. Builders establish construction schedules for the project and exercise control of the costs. Builders must be certain that all construction as outlined by the architect meets building codes, zoning laws, and environmental and safety standards. In some cases the builder also acts as the developer and has the tasks of obtaining financing for the construction and marketing the property after it is completed. About 32,300 people were active as residential builders in 1998.

Education and Background

All fifty states and the District of Columbia require architects to hold licenses before they can work without the supervision of a licensed architect. Although licensing requirements vary by state, to receive a license, an architect must generally hold a bachelor's degree in architecture and have three years of practical experience in the field or hold a master's degree and have two years experience in the field. The applicants also must pass a qualifying examination. It is legal to work in the architecture field without holding a license provided that you work under the supervision of a licensed architect. Many drafters and beginning workers do not have licenses. There are approximately 105 accredited schools in the United States that offer five-year bachelor's and six-year master's programs in architecture. Most of these programs are accredited by the National Architectural Accrediting Board, and the student should try to gain entry into an accredited program. Architects take courses that include design, engineering, urban planning, drafting, mathematics, and physics. Since architects spend a great deal of their time in design work, they must have some talent and creativity in analyzing and solving problems and be comfortable with computer systems.

Builders come to their field from a variety of areas. Many general contractors first worked as a subcontractor or worker in one of the specialized areas of the building trade such as carpentry, plumbing, or electrical. And in order to perform their jobs well, contractors should have a good working knowledge of all aspects of the construction process. However, much of the builder's job, especially if he or she also does at least part of the development of the project, involves costs analysis and control and administration of personnel. For this reason, builders should have a background in accounting, finance, and business practices. These skills may be acquired through work in a college degree program or individual courses in engineering, business, accounting, economics, and finance. Many colleges offer degrees in construction management. Courses in business, financial, and real estate law also can be helpful in understanding and complying with the many laws and regulations that cover building construction. A knowledge of the real estate market and of marketing techniques is essential for the builder who will sell his or her own properties after construction is completed.

Because a builder must work with many subcontractors, architects, and construction personnel, he or she must have strong communication skills and be able to coordinate and organize the work of many different people who are involved in the construction of the building. He or she must work well under pressure and be a good problem solver.

Working Conditions and Earnings

Architects spend much of their time in an office environment working on a computerized design program. Architects also talk to clients and contractors and discuss job requirements with engineers, landscape architects, and other involved parties. They may also visit the building site to oversee the work and be certain that no problems arise. Most architects work for architectural firms, builders, or developers. Some work for federal, state, and local agencies in community or housing departments. Many architects eventually become partners in existing firms or start their own firms. Although there are opportunities for architects throughout the country, many architectural jobs are located in large urban areas such as Los Angeles, Dallas, Chicago, and New York City. Architects often work long hours to complete projects, especially when they have their own firms.

Beginning architects may work as drafters drawing plans and creating models for projects. As they gain experience, architects may supervise the work of several drafters and take responsibility for the drawing for a project. Architects may specialize in design, material specifications, or testing of materials.

In 1998 the average salary for an architect was $47,710, according to the 1999 *Occupational Outlook Handbook*. After eight to ten years in practice, architects had median salaries of $54,700, according to the American Institute of Architects.

Builders generally divide their time between office work and visits to the building site. They may spend a great deal of their time on the telephone ordering various materials needed for the building. They may also maintain telephone contact with the supervisor at the site. Because they must visit the site and inspect the work, builders spend a portion of their time out-of-doors. They may also have to travel distances to reach a site.

Earnings for builders vary depending on the responsibilities they take for the project. According to the 1998 *Occupational Outlook Handbook*, the median annual salary for all construction managers was $47,610. A 2001 NACORE survey found that corporate construction managers averaged salaries of $113,631. Those who owned their own firms generally earned more than those who worked for developers, architects, or other firms. Because of the cyclical nature of the construction industry, there may be wide differences in the earnings of the builder from year to year.

Lawyers

Lawyers involved in real estate transactions may advise their clients on the legal implications of contracts, research regulations that may affect the project, examine the title to be certain that the property rights are not questionable, and advise investors on the legal obligations imposed by financing instruments. The lawyer may negotiate contracts for architects, builders, real estate agents, and other people and organizations concerned with a development.

In less populated areas of the country, attorneys may handle all types of legal work. In urban areas, attorneys have more of a tendency to specialize in one area such as corporate, real estate, tax, or criminal law. Lawyers who specialize in real estate transactions often work closely with real estate brokers and their clients in clarifying the details of the transactions and interpreting the laws relating to the properties. In the case of a large commercial development, attorneys may be involved in every stage of the project and will take the responsibility for negotiating all contracts and other legal papers involved in the transaction. For single-family home sales, the attorney may simply review the contract, prepare the deed, and check over the title evidence to be sure that the client's interest is protected.

Education and Background

In order to practice law in any state, the lawyer must pass the bar examination in that state or otherwise meet the requirements for the jurisdiction. In general a lawyer must retake the bar examination if he or she intends to practice in another state; however, there are exceptions. In most states, to qualify for the bar, applicants must have passed a three-year course of law after college at a school approved by the American Bar Association. A few states accept training in a law office instead of a college program. In law school the student will study contract law, property law, constitutional law, and judicial proceedings. In the last year of school the student may take courses that concentrate on one area of specialization. The student may also gain experience by working in the summer or on a part-time basis as a law clerk in an established firm.

Lawyers must have excellent research and writing skills to locate and communicate their opinions. Good analytical skills are necessary to draw conclusions and form opinions based on former law cases. The lawyer should be able to work well with clients and other attorneys in discussing the case and presenting opinions.

Working Conditions and Earnings

Many lawyers spend most of their work time in an office environment, although they may have to travel locally to work with clients, go to court, or attend real estate closings. Some lawyers work as employees or partners in law firms; others have individual practices. Many others work for federal, state, or local governments. Some attorneys may work for banks, corporations, or real estate firms, but in most cases the firm simply hires the services of a lawyer when they are needed. Many attorneys work long hours with considerable pressure, especially when a case is being tried. Hours may be irregular to meet the needs of clients. In general, attorneys who work for government agencies tend to have more regular work schedules than those working for private firms. To some extent lawyers can determine their own hours and workloads, depending on the number of clients they have. However, in general, the hours are longer than those for more conventional employees.

Beginning attorneys in private firms earned approximately $85,000 in 2000, although beginning salaries may vary depending upon the school the lawyer attended, academic standing and accomplishments, and the lawyer's specialization. Some lawyers in prestigious firms may have higher starting salaries. Salaries for experienced lawyers in private firms averaged over $120,000 a year in 2000. Partners in large firms generally earn more than sole practitioners.

Administrative Assistants and Clerical Personnel

Like those of almost any industry, real estate firms of every type employ administrative assistants, receptionists, and clerical personnel. In a real estate office, administrative assistants may be expected to type contracts and other legal forms involved in the sale of property. They also will have the responsibility of talking to clients and taking messages for salespeople who are often out of the office. Some successful real estate agents use personal assistants to handle routine clerical and client contact work so that the agents will have more time to make sales. Approximately 34 percent of all real estate firms employed personal assistants for salespeople in 1999, according to the *1999 NAR Profile of Real Estate Firms*. However, the 2001 NAR *Member Profile* found that only 20 percent of all agents use an assistant.

Administrative assistants may organize and disperse the information on new listings, open houses, and other activities of the real estate office. In some cases, he or she may use several kinds of data processing equipment to record and store information. The administrative assistant may also be responsible for directing marketing mailings to prospective clients and handling routine placement of advertising in local papers.

Education and Background

Although there are few specific entry requirements, administrative assistants and other clerical personnel in real estate offices should have good communications skills for working with clients as well as good organizational skills to keep track of the material that is used in listing and selling property. Since they often type legal contracts that must be completely accurate, good typing skills are essential. Familiarity with computer software and telecommunications skills are also essential in today's world of electronic listings and sales. An understanding of real estate terminology and legal terms is also helpful. Good mathematical skills may be needed to keep track of commission payments, earnest money deposits, rent payments, and other routine transactions. If personal assistants perform certain duties such as showing properties to buyers, they must have real estate licenses.

Working Conditions and Earnings

Real estate administrative assistants work in an office environment and usually work a regular forty-hour week. However, because real estate offices are often open in the evenings and on weekends, they may have to work during these periods. Real estate personal assistants who work for top-producing agents earn an average salary of $30,000, according to a recent NAR survey. As they acquire more knowledge of the business, administrative assistants may move into more demanding administrative positions, act as real estate closers, or study to become real estate sales agents.

Although license laws prohibit assistants from taking listings or performing other real estate sales activities, they often gain a great deal of knowledge about the field from working in an office. If they later decide to take the exam, this introduction to the field can be very valuable.

8

The Real Estate
Business Today

LIKE NEARLY EVERY other business in this country, the real estate industry has undergone major changes in the last thirty years. Although 60 percent of real estate firms are still small independent brokers operating from one or two offices and doing business on a local level, the picture is changing. Franchise operations have given local brokerage firms the advantage of a national identity. Regional multiple listing services and relocation services enable local firms to do business nationwide. In addition, the Internet has made it relatively easy for a small company to reach national and even international buyers and sellers. In the areas of commercial and large residential real estate, insurance companies, pension funds, REITs (real estate investment trusts), and banks are playing important roles as owners, sellers, and managers of office buildings, shopping centers, and apartment complexes.

Changes in the age, wealth, and location of the country's population also will have a major influence on the future of the real estate business. Population shifts from the Northeast and Midwest toward the South and the West continue to affect the demand for housing and commercial properties. And as the population of the United States gets older, its housing needs will change. Demand for vacation homes may increase as baby boomers start to retire. Immigration will be another major influence on housing demand. Approximately ten million people moved to the United States in the 1990s.

Changes in the availability of money to build and buy real estate and in the cost of that real estate also will affect the prosperity of the real estate business. As mortgage rates remain low, more and more people are able to afford a home, despite rising home prices. Government policies on the economy and on how taxes are levied against real estate owners will have a significant impact on the cost of home ownership and real estate investment.

Finally, the growing use of computers by real estate businesses will change the ways that real estate companies buy, sell, and finance the properties they handle. All of these factors will influence the business of real estate and the skills and training needed by the average real estate salesperson or broker for success in the years to come.

The Move Toward a National Real Estate Industry

Franchising

Franchising enjoyed rapid, continuous growth during most of the 1980s, but then it began to decline. The *1999 NAR Profile of Real Estate Firms* found that 22 percent of firms and 38 percent of the residential sales force were affiliated with franchises. Those numbers have been almost unchanged since 1996.

Real estate franchising is very concentrated, with a few organizations accounting for most of the market. In fact the top four real estate franchise organizations—Century 21, ERA, RE/MAX, and Coldwell Banker—account for most affiliated firms.

Franchises provide smaller real estate brokers with many of the same advantages enjoyed by national and regional firms. Franchises are able to afford larger national advertising budgets so that the franchise name (if not exactly that of the local broker) becomes well known. Like larger firms, franchises offer members training in management and sales techniques that can help them run their companies better. Many franchises also buy supplies such as contracts in quantity and pass the savings along to their members. Franchise firms also offer nationwide referral services that make it possible for local offices to provide relocation services to clients interested in real estate in other parts of the country.

Franchises have helped many smaller brokers who might otherwise have been unable to compete with large local firms. But the rapid growth of franchises has also resulted in many franchises taking as members firms that are unsuccessful and burdening their successful members with these not very competent coworkers. Likewise some franchises have failed to provide the professional assistance and materials that have been promised to members, making it more difficult for them to compete effectively.

Other Players in the National Real Estate Market

Even more than residential brokerage, the markets for office buildings, shopping centers, and multifamily apartments are developing national and international characters. In recent years national insurance companies, pension funds of large companies and unions, stock brokerage firms, and banks have renewed their commitments to own, sell, and manage real estate, both for themselves and for investors. Because many of these companies are large national firms, they have the resources needed to purchase and operate large commercial buildings. And these firms seldom limit their real estate activities to just one part of the country. This national involvement creates a better understanding of real estate market conditions in all parts of the country and helps to establish common practices and valuation techniques for investment real estate. The involvement of the Wall Street financial community in buying and selling interests in real estate, REITs (real estate investment trusts), and mortgages on real estate to investors also has helped to standardize real estate activities and to establish a national market for properties, regardless of where they are located.

Real estate investment trusts have been owners of real estate since the mid-1970s, but it was not until the mid-1990s that the current group of REIT owners gained prominence. Today REITs own approximately 11 percent of all real estate, including shopping centers, office buildings, apartments, warehouses, and hotels, as well as nursing homes and even prisons. Because REITs are corporations that buy and hold real estate for a long term, they offer many of the benefits of working in a corporate setting—pension funds, more extensive benefits, more job stability—than is usually available to small, independent companies.

The pension funds of large corporations and labor unions make up another group that continues to own a significant amount of real estate. In general, pension funds rely on real estate advisors to assist them in locating, purchasing, and operating their real estate.

Pension funds tend to favor investments in larger, more stable properties, but more aggressive funds will venture into development or more speculative purchases.

Wall Street also plays an indirect role in the real estate markets through the syndication of real estate mortgages. By buying mortgages from banks and then selling shares in the repayment of loan interests, the so-called secondary mortgage market helps make more funds available to purchase and build on properties.

A Changing Real Estate Climate

A Changing Population

The number of homes, offices, and shopping centers needed in any market depends in large part upon the composition of the population. The more people there are, the more houses will be needed for shelter, the more offices or factories will be needed to supply goods and services for them, and the more shopping malls will be needed to get those goods to the consumers.

One of the most important population trends that will influence real estate in the years ahead is the aging of the baby boom generation, born after World War II. The first baby boomers have turned fifty, and throughout the first part of the twenty-first century, the elderly population will grow significantly. Although some retirees move to warmer climates, the Census Bureau has determined that older people move less often than those younger than thirty-five. Many older citizens prefer to remain in their homes rather than move to smaller quarters or retirement facilities. The American Housing Survey found that almost three-quarters of seniors live in single-family homes and that 80 percent expect to remain there. Consequently, there may be less opportunity for home sales to these groups in the years ahead. However, vacation and second homes are increasingly popular with this group. Over 33 percent of those older than fifty-five plan to buy in either Florida or Arizona. The demand for retirement housing and assisted housing that provides some service to the elderly is expected to rise significantly after 2010.

At the same time, the children of the baby boomers will begin renting apartments and buying homes in the next decade. Most renters fall in the eighteen- to thirty-year-old range, so demand for rental apartments should increase in the years ahead. This means a greater demand for property managers.

Another major force that will significantly affect housing demand is the huge influx of immigration in the United States. Approximately 9 percent of the U.S. population was foreign-born in 1996, the highest level since 1930. Immigration is helping to offset any possible decline in housing demand over the next decade. However, as real estate agents prepare to serve these new home buyers, there are certain facts to keep in mind. According to the 1999 NAR report, *Housing in the New Millennium*, immigrant households tend to be larger than those of native-born residents; almost 23 percent of immigrants have five or more people in their households. In part because of this size, as well as for economic considerations, the Joint Center for Housing Studies at Harvard University has found that immigrant families are more likely to buy multifamily homes. Immigration is also concentrated on a few states and metropolitan areas, such as California, Texas, Florida, New York City, and Chicago. A longer-term result of increasing immigration will be a more diverse U.S. population. The U.S. Bureau of the Census projects that by 2020, Hispanics will account for more than 16 percent of the population, Asians will make up 6 percent, and African-Americans will account for just under 13 percent. For those active in the real estate profession, the ability to understand the needs and buying patterns of many different groups will be an important factor to success.

Many experts predict that a combination of a lower working-age population and a growth in telecommunicating and working at home will lower the demand for office buildings. Homes and apartments with room for home offices are very popular. However, early efforts at at-home work have already shown that people need to meet in offices for conferences, to work in teams, and to have social contact.

Although the demand for office space continues to be relatively strong, the type of space companies want does not remain constant. After more than a decade of moving office locations to low-rise suburban "office campuses," recent trends have shown that many companies are now returning to the central cities to find office space. Companies like the easy access to services central cities provide, and workers find it easier to reach jobs in downtown areas when there is good public transportation.

Some experts have also predicted that shopping by mail, on cable, and on the Web will soon replace the shopping mall. Even though some of the older malls built in the 1950s may become obsolete, malls remain an important center for social contact as well as shopping. The growth of cineplexes, theme restaurants, and service businesses in many malls also supports the idea of "mall as town center."

Indeed, some of the newer shopping centers are actually being constructed like old-fashioned downtowns, with sidewalks, individually designed storefronts and signs for businesses, and streets running through the center. The trend appears to be working. According to the International Council of Shopping Centers, more than 197 million adults visited shopping centers in 2000 and bought more than $1.14 trillion in goods and services.

Although the appearance and even the function of homes, offices, and malls may change in the future, there will still be a need for real estate and for those who buy, sell, build, and lease it.

A Changing Financial and Economic Climate

The growth and direction of the real estate industry also depends upon the strength of the economy and on the availability of financing to build and buy property. In a reaction to the overly free lending of the 1980s, today's lenders continue to use fairly stringent guidelines in making loans. Commercial borrowers must put up significantly higher portions of the construction costs than were required at that time. Banks also must meet stricter federal guidelines on real estate lending, which makes it more difficult to obtain a loan. Most experts believe that this stricter lending climate has had a long-term benefit for the real estate industry because it has kept developers from building more buildings than people needed, as happened in the 1980s.

Today's lower interest rates have made it easier for people to afford to build and buy homes and commercial buildings. However, concerns about a recession could again cause interest rates to rise and create problems for the prosperity of the real estate markets.

In recent years several factors have contributed to making money more available for real estate activity. The introduction of the computer network, and now of the Internet, have made it possible for lenders and buyers to track interest rates worldwide and have relatively easy access to money. If your bank does not have money for a loan, perhaps a bank in another state or another country has the funds at a more favorable rate. Real estate finance is no longer restricted by location.

A stronger market for the resale of real estate loans is also helping to provide more money for real estate. For a long time, residential mortgages have been grouped together and sold on what is called the "secondary market." Investors buy the rights to the interest a home buyer pays, and banks obtain new funds to make new loans.

Recent regulations changes have made it much easier to conduct similar secondary sales of mortgages for large commercial buildings. Thus, many experts hope that money will be easier to obtain for real estate construction and purchase. In turn this available money should help to keep real estate from experiencing the sharp up and down cycles in value that it has traditionally known.

New sources of funds for real estate also have come from pension funds and insurance companies, who have been actively investing in real estate for the last fifteen years. These companies obtain their money from company and personal retirement accounts and premiums on life insurance. At first, most pension funds and insurers invested only in larger commercial buildings, but in recent years, they have been more active in financing multifamily and single-family homes.

Another source of funding that has become increasingly important to real estate is public money. Real estate companies for real estate investment trusts (REITs) sell shares in their real estate holdings on the stock market. The companies then use the money from these shares to build, improve, or buy real estate. Although REITs have been around for several decades, their importance has increased dramatically since the early 1990s.

The Growth of Technology

Today the use of the Web to show and sell properties represents the future of real estate. Already many companies large and small have home pages to market their properties and their real estate services. Digital cameras enable sales agents to include photographs of new properties on their sites. Mapping programs permit users to see where the properties are located. Prospective buyers can even have a "virtual tour" of the property online, viewing different rooms as if they were actually there. Multiple listing services where many properties can be evaluated and viewed also are making extensive use of the Internet. Other Internet sites allow buyers to research homes online and sellers to contact buyers directly through the Web.

As transactions on the Web become more secure, many predict that actual sales of real estate, including viewing, obtaining, financing, and signing of the papers, will soon occur over the Web. Several groups, including the NAR, continue to work to develop "transaction platforms" for just that purpose. However, it seems unlikely that with the huge variety of housing available, people will be willing to make such a large purchase without seeing the property in person.

Buying and selling property still requires specialized knowledge few possess, so the demand for real estate agents seems secure.

The Future of Real Estate

Real estate—like every other business—has been changed by the technological advances of the late twentieth century. The Internet, the cellular phone, and the digital camera have made it possible for real estate salespeople to communicate with buyers, sellers, and investors more quickly and efficiently. It's now easily possible for a buyer to view a property online, negotiate a price via E-mail, and secure a mortgage online. Many large real estate companies, as well as associations such as the National Association of REAL-TORS, are currently working toward a time when the entire real estate sale—including signing the contract with an e-signature, could be handled online. Some experts believe that when this day arrives, the demand for real estate agents and related real estate professionals will decline. Already, according to an NAR survey, 39 percent of home buyers used the Internet to research their choices.

Although technology will definitely change the way real estate is bought and sold, most buyers are eager for the advice, support, and assistance a trained real estate professional can provide. Sophisticated commercial buyers soon may be comfortable buying a building they have never seen in person, but most home owners will still want to see, touch, and feel what the place they might call home looks like. And they will continue to want the help of a real estate agent as they make the biggest purchase of their lives.

Appendix A

Real Estate–Related Associations

The following is not a complete list of all associations related to real estate, but it will give those interested in the field a good way to learn more. Use the websites provided for each association to get details quickly.

American Bankers Association
1120 Connecticut Avenue NW
Washington, D.C. 20036
aba.com

American Builders and Contractors Association
1300 North Seventeenth Street
Rosslyn, VA 22209
abc.org

American Institute of Contractors
466 Ninety-Fourth Avenue N
St. Petersburg, FL 33702
aicnet.org

American Land Title Association
1828 L Street NW
Washington, D.C. 20036
alta.org

American Planning Association
176 Massachusetts Avenue NW
Washington, D.C. 20036
planning.org

American Real Estate and Urban Economics Association
Indiana University
Kelley School of Business
1309 East Tenth Street
Bloomington, IN 47495
areuea.org

American Resort Development Association
1220 L Street NW
Washington, D.C. 20005
arda.org

American Society of Appraisers
555 Herndon Parkway
Herndon, VA 20107
appraisers.org

The Appraisal Institute
875 North Michigan Avenue
Chicago, IL 60611
appraisalinstitute.org

Appraisal Institute of Canada
111 Portage Avenue
Winnipeg, Manitoba
Canada R3G 0S8
aicanada.org

The Association of Real Estate License Law Officials
P.O. Box 23105
Montgomery, AL 36123
arello.org

Building Owners and Managers Association
1201 New York Avenue NW
Washington, D.C. 20005
boma.org

Canadian Real Estate Association
344 Slater Street
Ottawa, Ontario
Canada K1R 7Y3
crea.ca

CCIM Institute
430 North Michigan Avenue
Chicago, IL 60611
ccim.org

Community Associations Institute
1423 Powhata Street
Alexandria, VA 22317
cai.org

The Counselors of Real Estate
430 North Michigan Avenue
Chicago, IL 60611
cre.org

The Industrial Development Research Council
35 Technology Parkway
Norcross, GA 30092
idrc.org

The Institute of Real Estate Management
430 North Michigan Avenue
Chicago, IL 60611
irem.org

International Council of Shopping Centers
1221 Avenue of the Americas
New York, NY 10022
icsc.org

International Facility Management Association
1 East Greenway Plaza
Houston, TX 77046
ifma.org

Mortgage Bankers Association of America
1919 Pennsylvania Avenue
Washington D.C. 20006
mba.org

National Apartment Association
201 North Union Street
Alexandria, VA 22314
naahq.org

National Association of Exclusive Buyer Agents
320 West Sabai Palm Place
Longwood, FL 32779
naeba.com

National Association of Home Builders
1201 Fifteenth Street NW
Washington, D.C. 20005
nahb.org

National Association of Office and Industrial Parks
2201 Cooperative Way
Herndon, VA 20171
naiop.org

National Association of Real Estate Investment Trusts
1129 Twentieth Street NW
Washington, D.C. 20036
nareit.org

National Association of Realtors
430 North Michigan Avenue
Chicago, IL 60611
realtor.org

National Association of Residential Property Managers
P.O. Box 140647
Austin, TX 78714
narpm.org

National Association of Review Appraisers and Mortgage Underwriters
1224 North Nokomis NNE
Alexandria, VA 56308
iami.org

National Auctioneer Association
8880 Ballentine
Overland Park, KS 66204
auctioneers.org

National Multihousing Council
1850 M Street NW
Washington, D.C. 20036
nmhc.org

National Realty Committee
1420 New York Avenue NW
Washington, D.C. 20005
realestateroundtable.com

Pension Real Estate Association
95 Glastonbury Road
Glastonbury, CT 06033
prea.org

Real Estate Brokerage Managers Council
430 North Michigan Avenue
Chicago, IL 60611
crb.org

Real Estate Institute of Canada
5407 Eglinton Avenue W
Toronto, Ontario
Canada M9C 5K6
reic.com

Realtors Land Institute
430 North Michigan Avenue
Chicago, IL 60611
rliland.com

Residential Sales Council
430 North Michigan Avenue
Chicago, IL 60611
rsb.org

Society of Industrial and Office Realtors
70012 Eleventh Street NW
Washington, D.C. 20001
sior.org

Urban Land Institute
1025 Thomas Jefferson Street NW
Washington, D.C. 20007
uli.org

Schools Offering Real Estate Courses

THE FOLLOWING IS a partial list of universities offering real estate degree or major programs. Many community colleges and private schools also offer real estate courses, especially those required to obtain a real estate license. Lists of schools offering real estate education are also available at the websites of the Association of Real Estate License Law Officials (arello.org) and the National Association of Office and Industrial Parks (naiop.org/career/center).

Arizona State University
College of Architecture and Environmental Design
Tempe, AZ 85287
asu.edu

Babson College
Department of Finance
Forest Street
Babson Park, MA 02154
babson.edu

University of British Columbia
Commerce and Business Administration
2053 Main Mall
Vancouver, British Columbia
Canada V6T IZ2
commerce.ubc.ca

California State University, Northridge
College of Business Administration
1811 Nordhoff Street
Northridge, CA 91330
csun.edu

University of California at Berkeley
Fisher Center for Real Estate and Urban Economics
Haas School of Business
602 Faculty Building
Berkeley, CA 94720
groups.haas.berkeley.edu/realestate

University of Cincinnati
College of Business Administration
403 Carl H. Lindner Hall
Cincinnati, OH 45521
uc.edu

Cleveland State University
Department of Finance
James J. Nancy College of Business
1737 Euclid Avenue
Cleveland, OH 44115
csuohio.edu

Colorado State University
Department of Real Estate
College of Business
Fort Collins, CO 80523
colostate.edu

University of Colorado
College of Business
Campus Box 419
Boulder, CO 80309
colorado.edu

Columbia University
Real Estate Development
Graduate School of Architecture and Planning
409 Avery Hall
New York, NY 10027
columbia.edu

University of Connecticut
Center for Real Estate
U-41RE
368 Fairfield Road
Storrs, CT 06269
uconn.edu

Cornell University
Program in Real Estate
219 West Sibley Hall
Ithaca, NY 14850
cornell.edu

University of Denver
School of Real Estate
2199 West University Boulevard
Denver, CO 80208
dcb.du.edu

Florida Atlantic University
Finance and Real Estate
777 Glades Road
Boca Raton, FL 33431
fau.edu

Florida State University
Department of Insurance and Real Estate
College of Business
Tallahassee, FL 32306
cob.fsu.edu

University of Florida
Warrington College of Business Administration
Box 117168
Gainesville, FL 32611
cba.ufl.edu

George Washington University
Department of Finance
101 Lisner Hall
2023 G Street NW
Washington, D.C. 20052
gwu.edu

Georgia State University
Department of Real Estate
College of Business Administration
P.O. Box 4020
Atlanta, GA 30302
gsu.edu

University of Georgia
Department of Insurance, Legal Studies,
    Real Estate, and Management Science
206 Brooks Hall
Athens, GA 30602
uga.edu/realestate/

University of Hartford
Barney School of Business
2000 Bloomfield Avenue
West Hartford, CT 06117
hartford.edu

Harvard University
Graduate School of Design
48 Quincy Street
Cambridge, MA 02138
gsd.harvard.edu

University of Hawaii
Honolulu, HI 96817
hawaii.edu

University of Illinois at Champaign-Urbana
Department of Finance
1206 South Sixth Street
Champaign, IL 61820
uiuc.edu

Indiana University
Kelley School of Business
1309 Tenth Street
Bloomington, IN 47405
indiana.edu

Johns Hopkins University
Allan L. Berman Real Estate Center
One Charles Plaza
Charles and Saratoga Streets
Baltimore, MD 21201
spsbe.jhu.edu

Lehigh University
Rauch Business Center
Bethlehem, PA 18015
lehigh.edu

Louisiana State University
Department of Finance
2164 CEBA
Baton Rouge, LA 70803
lsu.edu

Massachusetts Institute of Technology
Center for Real Estate
77 Massachusetts Avenue
Cambridge, MA 02139
mit.edu

University of Michigan
Department of Finance and Real Estate
701 Tappan Street
Ann Arbor, MI 48109
umich.edu

Mississippi State University
msstate.edu

University of Mississippi
bus.olemiss.edu

University of Missouri
business.missouri.edu

Morehead State University
301 Howell-McDowell Road
Morehead, KY 40351
morehead-st.edu

University of Nebraska
Real Estate and Land Use
Omaha, NE 68182
unomaha.edu

University of Nevada
Las Vegas, NV 89557
nevada.edu

University of New Orleans
College of Business
Lake Front Campus
New Orleans, LA 70148
uno.edu

New York University
The Real Estate Institute
11 West Forty-Second Street
New York, NY 10036
stern.nyu.edu

University of North Carolina–Chapel Hill
Kenan Flagler School of Business
CB #3410
Chapel Hill, NC 27599
unc.edu

Northwestern University
Kellogg Graduate School
Leverone/Anderson Hall, Room 4-080
2001 Sheridan Road
Evanston, IL 60208
kellogg.nwu.edu

The Ohio State University
255 Fisher Hall
2100 Neil Avenue
Columbus, OH 43210
fisher.osu.edu

Pennsylvania State University
Department of Insurance and Real Estate
Smeal College of Business
409 Business Administration Building
University Park, PA 16802
psu.edu

University of Pennsylvania
The Wharton School of Business
256 South Thirty-Seventh Street
Philadelphia, PA 19104
wharton.upenn.edu

University of Quebec
Real Estate Program (Module d'Affairs
    Immobilieres)
Department of Administrative Sciences
    (Department des Sciences Administratives)
P.O. Box 6192, Station A
Montreal, Quebec
Canada H3C 3P8

Rutgers University
33 Livingston Avenue
New Brunswick, NJ 08901
rutgers.edu

University of San Diego
College of Business Administration
SS3350
San Diego, CA 91282
usdbusiness.ucsusd.edu

University of South Carolina
Darla Moor School of Business
Columbia, SC 29208
sc.edu

University of Southern California
Program in Real Estate
331 Ralph and Goldy Lewis Hall
Los Angeles, CA 90089
usc.edu

University of Southern Maine
68 High Street
Portland, ME 04101
usm.maine.edu

Southern Methodist University
Department of Finance, Insurance, and Real Estate
Edwin L. Cox School of Business
440 Fincher Building
Dallas, TX 75275
reil.cox.smu.edu

Southern Polytechnic State University
Environmental Development
School of Architecture
1100 South Marietta Parkway
Marietta, GA 30060
spsu.edu

Texas A&M University
Land Economics and Real Estate
Graduate School of Business
College Station, TX 77843
tamu.edu

University of Texas at Austin
Department of Finance
Graduate School of Business
Austin, TX 78712
bus.utex.edu

University of Toledo
College of Business Administration
Toledo, OH 43606
utoledo.edu

Virginia Commonwealth University
Real Estate and Urban Land Development
School of Business
Box 844000
1015 Floyd Avenue
Richmond, VA 23284
bsu.vcu.edu/finance

Virginia Tech
Blacksburg, VA 24601
vt.edu

Washington State University
Box 644861
Pullman, WA 99164
wsu.edu

University of West Florida
College of Business
11000 University Highway
Pensacola, FL 32514
uwf.edu

University of Western Ontario
Urban Development Program
Social Science Center
London, Ontario
Canada N6A 5C2
uwo.ca

University of Wisconsin at Madison
Real Estate Department
School of Business
975 University Avenue
Madison, WI 53706
wisc.edu/bschool

York University
Program in Real Property
Schulich School of Business
4700 Keele Street
North York, Ontario
Canada M3J 1P3
yorku.ca

Appendix C

Suggested Reading

THE FOLLOWING IS a partial list of publications that can be helpful to the person considering a career in real estate. Check out websites such as amazon.com and barnesandnoble.com for new books in this field.

Career Manuals

Burgess, Russell. *Real Estate Home Inspection*. Chicago: Real Estate Education Company, 1998.

Cross, Carla. *How About a Career in Real Estate?* Chicago: Dearborn Financial Publishing, 1993.

Edwards, Kenneth. *Your Successful Real Estate Career*. New York: AMACOM, 1997.

Evans, Blanche. *The Hottest E-Careers in Real Estate*. Chicago: Dearborn Publishing, 2001.

Janik, Carolyn, and Ruth Rejnis. *Real Estate Careers: Twenty-Five Growth Opportunities for Good Times and Bad*. New York: Wiley, 1994.

Masi, Mary, and Lauren Starkey. *Real Estate Career Starter.* New
    York: Learning Express, 2001.
National Association of REALTORS. *Careers in Real Estate.*
    Available online at nar.realtor.com.
Quinlan, Kathleen. *Real Estate Sales Agent.* Minnetonka, MN:
    Capstone Press, 1999.
Robinson, Maxx, et al. *So You Want to Go into Real Estate?* Cardi-
    nal Books, 1999.

Examination Guides

AMP Real Estate Sales Exam. New York: Learning Express, 1998.
ASI Real Estate Sales Exam. New York: Learning Express, 1998.
Beck, John. *Guide to the ASI Real Estate License Examination.*
    Upper Saddle River, NJ: Prentice Hall, 2001.
Coleman, David, et al. *Real Estate Math.* Chicago: Real Estate
    Education Company, 1997.
Fisher, Jeffrey, and Dennis Tosh. *Questions and Answers to Help
    you Pass the Real Estate Appraisal Exam.* Chicago: Dearborn
    Trade Publishing, 2000.
Gaddy, Wade E., Jr. *AL Study Guide for Real Estate Fundamentals.*
    Chicago: Dearborn Financial Publishing, 1994.
Garton-Good, Julie. *Real Estate Licensing Supercourse,* 2nd ed.
    New York: Arco Publishing, 1995.
Pivar, William. *California Real Estate License Prep.* Chicago: Real
    Estate Education Company, 2001.
Pivar, William. *Real Estate Exam Guide Designed for ASI Sales
    and Broker Exams.* Chicago: Real Estate Education Com-
    pany, 2000.
PSI Real Estate Sales Exam. New York: Learning Express, 1998.

Reilly, John, and Paige Vitousk. *Questions and Answers to Help You Pass the Real Estate Examination.* Chicago: Real Estate Education Company, 2000.

Sager, Lawrence, and Joyce Sterling. *Guide to Passing the PSI Real Estate Exam,* 2nd ed. Chicago: Dearborn Financial Publishing, 2000.

Sterling, Joyce. *Your Guide to Passing the AMP Real Estate Exam,* 2nd ed. Chicago: Dearborn Publishing, 1999.

Texas Real Estate Sales Exam. New York: Learning Express, 2000.

Real Estate Fundamentals

Boog, Bob. *Selling Homes 1-2-3.* THS International, 1998.

Breckenridge, Karl. *Fast Start in Real Estate.* Chicago: Dearborn Financial Publishing, 1992.

Cross, Carla. *The Real Estate Agent's Business Planning Guide.* Chicago: Dearborn Financial Publishing, 1994.

Gaddy, Wade, Jr., and Robert Hart. *Real Estate Fundamentals,* 4th ed. Chicago: Dearborn Financial Publishing, 1996.

Galaty, Filmore, et al. *Modern Real Estate Practice,* 15th ed. Chicago: Dearborn Financial Publishing, 1999.

Geltner, David, and Norman Miller. *Commercial Real Estate Analysis and Investments.* Cincinnati, OH: South-Western Publishing, 2000.

Griswold, Robert. *Property Management for Dummies.* New York: Hungry Minds, Inc., 2001.

Harwood, Bruce. *Real Estate Introduction.* Upper Saddle River, NJ: Prentice Hall, 2001.

Jacobus, Charles. *Real Estate Principles,* 8th ed. Cincinnati, OH: South-Western Publishing, 1999.

Kennedy, Danielle, and Warren Jamison. *How to List and Sell Real Estate in the 21st Century*. Chicago: Dearborn Financial Publishing, 2000.

Martin, Stephen, and Thomas Battle. *The Guide to Real Estate*. Eagan, MN: West Legal Services, 2000.

McKenzie, Dennis. *California Real Estate Principles*, 4th ed. Chicago: Dearborn Financial Publishing, 2001.

Rudman, Jack. *Handbook of Real Estate Terms*. Upper Saddle River, NJ: Prentice Hall, 1991.

Shlaes, Jared. *Real Estate Counseling in a Plain Brown Wrapper*. American Society of Real Estate, 1992.

Tyson, Erick, and Ray Brown. *House Selling for Dummies*. New York: Hungry Minds, Inc., 1997.

Van Reken, Randall, and Sandra Byrd. *Real Estate: Learning the Practices of the Professional*. Upper Saddle River, NJ: Prentice Hall, 1997.

Ventolo, William, and Martha Williams. *Fundamentals of Real Estate Appraisal*. Chicago: Dearborn Financial Publishing, 2001.

Wofford, Larry E., and Terrance M. Clauretie. *Real Estate,* 3rd ed. New York: Wiley, 1992.

About the Author

Mariwyn Evans graduated from Vanderbilt University in Nashville, Tennessee. She has written and edited several books on real estate including *Modern Real Estate Practice*, the *Virginia* and *Alabama Supplements for Modern Real Estate Practice, How About a Career in Real Estate?*, and *Profits from Real Estate Publicity*, done in conjunction with Howard S. Bimson. She has also helped to develop manuals used in teaching real estate principles and practices and real estate finance. She was the executive editor of the *Journal of Property Management*, the official publication of the Institute of Real Estate Management in Chicago, Illinois, for seventeen years. She is currently a Web editor for the online magazine published by the National Association of REALTORS, realtormag.com.